CYBER MOBS

DESTRUCTIVE ONLINE COMMUNITIES

By Allison Krumsiek

LUCENT
PRESS

Published in 2018 by
Lucent Press, an Imprint of Greenhaven Publishing, LLC
353 3rd Avenue
Suite 255
New York, NY 10010

Designer: Seth Hughes
Editor:Jennifer Lombardo

Cataloging-in-Publication Data

Names: Krumsiek, Allison.
Title: Cyber mobs: destructive online communities / Allison Krumsiek.
Description: New York : Lucent Press, 2018. | Series: Hot topics | Includes index.
Identifiers: ISBN 9781534561533 (library bound) | ISBN 9781534561540 (ebook)
Subjects: LCSH: Cyberbullying–Juvenile literature. | Online trolling–Juvenile literature.
Classification: LCC HV6773.15.C92 K78 2018 | DDC 302.34'302854678–dc23

Printed in the United States of America

CPSIA compliance information: Batch #BS17KL: For further information contact Greenhaven Publishing LLC, New York, New York at 1-844-317-7404.

Please visit our website, www.greenhavenpublishing.com. For a free color catalog of all our
high-quality books, call toll free 1-844-317-7404 or fax 1-844-317-7405.

CONTENTS

Adolescence is a time when many people begin to take notice of the world around them. News channels, blogs, and talk radio shows are constantly promoting one view or another; very few are unbiased. Young people also hear conflicting information from parents, friends, teachers, and acquaintances. Often, they will hear only one side of an issue or be given flawed information. People who are trying to support a particular viewpoint may cite inaccurate facts and statistics on their blogs, and news programs present many conflicting views of important issues in our society. In a world where it seems everyone has a platform to share their thoughts, it can be difficult to find unbiased, accurate information about important issues.

It is not only facts that are important. In blog posts, in comments on online videos, and on talk shows, people will share opinions that are not necessarily true or false, but can still have a strong impact. For example, many young people struggle with their body image. Seeing or hearing negative comments about particular body types online can have a huge effect on the way someone views himself or herself and may lead to depression and anxiety. Although it is important not to keep information hidden from young people under the guise of protecting them, it is equally important to offer encouragement on issues that affect their mental health.

The titles in the Hot Topics series provide readers with different viewpoints on important issues in today's society. Many of these issues, such as teen pregnancy and Internet safety, are of immediate concern to young people. This series aims to give readers factual context on these crucial topics in a way that lets them form their own opinions. The facts presented throughout also serve to empower readers to help themselves or support people they know who are struggling with many of the challenges adolescents face today. Although negative viewpoints are not ignored or downplayed, this series allows young people to see that the challenges they face are not insurmountable. Eating disorders can be overcome, the Internet can be navigated safely, and pregnant teens do not have to feel hopeless.

Quotes encompassing all viewpoints are presented and cited so readers can trace them back to their original source, verifying for themselves whether the information comes from a reputable place. Additional books and websites are listed, giving readers a starting point from which to continue their own research. Chapter questions encourage discussion, allowing young people to hear and understand their classmates' points of view as they further solidify their own. Full-color photographs and enlightening charts provide a deeper understanding of the topics at hand. All of these features augment the informative text, helping young people understand the world they live in and formulate their own opinions concerning the best way they can improve it.

When Socialization Goes Wrong

Human beings are social by nature. They like to belong to groups. Since the time of the earliest human beings, people have formed groups to protect and help each other. These groups often worked together for the good of society to get things done. People share information with each other and create a feeling of connection. This is how everyone makes friends.

People belong to a number of groups at one time, including friend groups, neighborhoods, fans of specific sports teams or television shows, religions, and countries. These groups generally share their ideas with each other. John Stuart Mill, one of the first philosophers to look at government, believed that the liberty to speak ideas was connected to the ability to think. If speech was restricted, then ideas would be restricted. Freedom of ideas helps keep groups healthy. To create a better society, Mill believed free speech was important. He also thought certain speech should not be protected: Speech that causes harm was not essential to liberty, Mill believed.

In the United States, the Constitution gives everyone the right to freedom of speech. The Founding Fathers, who wrote the Constitution, had read Mill's works. They protected speech except when it causes harm to other people. They believed, like Mill, that freedom of information and ideas was important for a healthy society. They created a society where information could be shared by anyone and people had the right to gather in groups to talk about their ideas. The United States still follows these ideas of freedom of speech and assembly. However, in recent years, many have wondered how these rules work on the Internet.

The Internet changed a lot of the ways people form groups and share ideas. Information spread around the world but not as quickly

The United States Constitution protects free speech, even on the Internet, but lawmakers are trying to figure out the best way to do this while still keeping people safe.

as it does today. People could write books, letters, pamphlets, or posters to document their ideas. These ideas could then be sent in the mail to other people or published and made available in bookstores or libraries.

Today, millions of people worldwide have instant access to the ideas of others. People can also form groups instantly, and their members can include people all around the world. This freedom to form groups is wonderful for many reasons, but it can also have negative consequences. In certain groups, belonging means being cruel to another person or excluding other people. Groups that form quickly to harass or bully another person are called mobs. Dr. Heinz Leymann, a Swedish researcher, identified this behavior in workplaces. "Psychical terror or mobbing in working life," wrote Leymann, "means hostile and unethical communication which is directed in a systematic way by one or a number of persons mainly toward one individual."[1] This behavior is not restricted to workplaces; any group of people can begin mobbing by harassing someone outside their group.

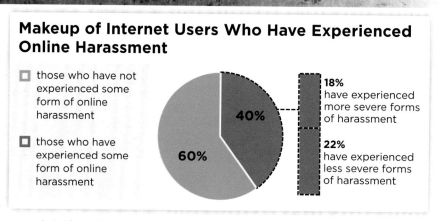

Makeup of Internet Users Who Have Experienced Online Harassment

☐ those who have not experienced some form of online harassment

☐ those who have experienced some form of online harassment

40%

60%

18% have experienced more severe forms of harassment

22% have experienced less severe forms of harassment

Nearly half of all Internet users report experiencing online harassment, according to this information from the Pew Research Center.

There are many types of mobs. Some mobs may have a positive purpose, such as dance mobs or flash mobs that gather for entertainment. It is easier than ever for people to organize quickly around an idea. New technological advancements, such as social media platforms, allow online groups to form almost in an instant. Groups may form to create positive social change or to cause destruction and chaos. After a sports win or a loss, fans may come together in a mob to overturn cars or burn areas of the town, sometimes turning a positive event into something negative. Historically in the United States, lynch mobs came together to target black individuals, often leading to the death of the targeted person.

In the online world, groups that gather together quickly around an idea and produce negative consequences are called cyber mobs. On the Internet, bullies can gather with other like-minded people and silence individuals or whole groups of people very quickly. Cyber mobs often use threats of real violence, online rumors and lies, and attacks on technology to scare their targets.

A Permanent Record

Information, true or false, never truly goes away after it has been put on the Internet. Even if it is deleted, it can often be retrieved by a dedicated person with the right skills. If a report includes a person's name, it will come up any time someone searches for that person online. This can cause embarrassment or worse, such as job loss or loss of trust from other people. It can be hard to overcome mistakes, and the Internet sometimes makes it impossible for anyone to forget people's worst moments.

Cyber mobs use this permanent record to try to make people afraid. Some of the tactics for harassment include stealing and publishing personal information, altering photos of the victim or their family, e-mailing threats to a victim's employer, filing false police reports, and using the permanence of the Internet to plant damaging information about victims.

False information about these victims can impact their lives forever. Future employers, schools, or partners will be able to find information posted online and may believe the false information is true. Victims of cyber mobs sometimes try to stop using the Internet completely or not use their real name online. By not using the Internet, these victims lose vital connections to friends, jobs, and other opportunities.

The Internet is still relatively new, and it changes all the time. Laws often have not kept pace with it. Even when new laws are passed, police officers may not be up to date on current laws and think they are unable to help victims. Many victims believe no one can help them stop the abuse of a cyber mob. However, as Danielle Citron, author of *Hate Crimes in Cyberspace,* wrote, "Victims cannot and should not have to wrestle with cyber harassment on their own."[2] In recent years, many civil rights groups have formed to help victims of cyber abuse. These online help groups work to counter hate speech online, provide resources for victims, work to change the laws, and train police officers on how to help.

The Internet was created to be an open place for all people to share their ideas and learn from each other. However, just like in the rest of the world, any gathering of people may have its bullies. According to a report by the Data Society, more than 40 percent of Internet users have experienced harassment online.

The behavior of cyber mobs and of people who fight back is changing the Internet. Cyber mobs are able to find personal information faster than ever before. They can target a person quickly and use scary tactics to intimidate someone. However, at the same time, new methods are helping victims come together and are being used to train lawyers and law enforcement to help stop cyber mobs. These forces are working at the same time all over the world.

CHAPTER 1

The Rise of Cyber Mobs

More than 3.2 billion people were online in 2015, up from 738 million in 2000. Around 40 percent of the global population has an Internet connection, and this allows people from all over the world to communicate and learn new things. It can help them share ideas, make friends, and get jobs or an education.

Groups on the Internet are often created around similarities, including love of a common television show, musical group, or entertainer. Support groups are also formed on the Internet for people facing challenges such as cancer or the loss of a loved one. However, the Internet also introduces people to ideas they may not like or people they do not agree with. Sometimes, people misuse this connection to harass those they do not agree with. Often, people on the Internet are harassed for the things they enjoy or simply for who they are. Entertainers and people in the public eye are often targets of harassment as well. Many people do not feel safe sharing their ideas on the Internet because of this bullying.

The feelings of fear, embarrassment, or pain that come from being bullied are the same whether the bullying is offline or online. The difference with cyberbullying is that it is not as easy as walking away to stop the attack. With cyberbullying, the abuse can follow someone wherever they go; the bully does not need to be physically present to make an impact.

Cyberbullying can also be repeated more often than regular bullying. If a bully in school writes a mean note to a target, the target can throw the note away, and although the bully can write a new one, they have certain limitations. In contrast, mean notes on the Internet can be passed around forever, reproduced quickly, and brought back after being deleted. The same can happen with photos or videos. A cyber mob may take an embarrassing video of a victim and continue the harassment by posting it to different websites. New members of cyber mobs may discover the video years later and start the harassment all over again.

Bullying can take place both online and offline. Cyberbullying is often harder to get away from and can involve social media, text messages, e-mails, or other forms of online communication.

This kind of harassment and bullying can be unintended. A friend might take a funny or embarrassing photo of another friend and send it to them. Although both friends would know this was a joke, the image could be stolen by someone who was not in on the joke. It could then be used to bully and harass the subject of the picture. The bully may post the photo on multiple websites. Anyone who helps spread the photo becomes part of the cyber mob. This can include friends of the victim as well as people who do not even know the person. In legal terms, these bystanders become accessories to any crime that happens. This does not apply to people who try to help by sending the photo to teachers, parents, or the police, only to people who share it in an effort to hurt the victim. Some people may not even realize they are doing this; they may share the photo because they think it is funny, not thinking about the fact that the subject of the photo is a real person with real feelings. This is called dehumanizing, and it makes it easier for people to be cruel. Dehumanizing can happen either by accident or on purpose.

Words shared on the Internet are protected by freedom of speech in many countries, as well as by the United Nations (UN). Even hateful or harassing speech may be protected. It is a difficult balance for online communities to give everyone a right to their ideas while protecting vulnerable groups from harassment. There are many ways the Internet and even freedom of speech laws have helped the rise of harassment in the form of cyber mobs.

How Cyber Mobs Form

Participation in a cyber mob is considered bullying behavior. Bullies exist in all communities, online and offline. Someone who is a bully may threaten a victim either physically or verbally. Bullies will often spread rumors, or untrue information, about a victim. They will sometimes act nice to a victim to get the victim to tell them a secret or embarrassing information. Later, the bullies will use that information against the victim.

Bullies online tend to seek out communities of other bullies. If someone who does not like another group of people finds a community of people who believe the same things they do, it can be easy for them to spread hateful information. In online communities, the bully may not even know the victim. They may not have anything personally against the victim, but a group may be able to convince others that the person deserves to be bullied for some reason. This may be because of skin color, gender, sexual orientation, or something the victim did that the group is reacting to in an inappropriately severe way. A group of people who attack other people can begin to think and act as a group even without ever seeing each other. They might temporarily forget their own ideas and follow the leader. This is called a mob mentality. The website No Bullying defines it as "a group effort to attack an individual through methods of intimidation, isolation, and humiliation."[3]

Another term for this mob mentality is groupthink. The term was coined by social psychologist Irving Janis and refers to groups that make bad decisions under social pressure. Janis studied groups and concluded that the social pressures in a group may lead individuals to act in immoral ways. The participants in a cyber mob form opinions based on unchallenged assumptions. They may think the target of their hate is bad because the rest of the group does. Even if someone challenges that idea, they may ignore certain facts rather than admit they may have been wrong. Individuals involved in groupthink believe they are right even when shown evidence and arguments to prove they are not, and they use this sense of righteousness to excuse bad behavior. Groupthink can lead individuals to ignore the negative consequences of their actions and stereotype anyone outside the group as an enemy. When group members think they are right at all costs and that anyone who believes otherwise is an enemy, they can make dangerous decisions. Individuals within the group also have to be careful. In groupthink, there is no room for people to question the beliefs of the group. Individuals who begin to doubt the actions of the group may become targets themselves.

UNDERSTANDING IS KEY

"The impulse to gang up, to join with others against what is perceived to be a common threat, lies deep in human nature. It is not easily outlawed … The better we understand ourselves, including our darker impulses, the more able we are to keep one another healthy and safe."
–Kenneth Westhues, professor of sociology at the University of Waterloo

Kenneth Westhues, "At the Mercy of the Mob," OHS Canada, vol. 18, no. 8, December 2002, pp. 30–36. www.kwesthues.com/ohs-canada.htm.

On the Internet, it is easier for people to fall into the mob mentality. Some scientists believe that joining certain online communities makes it easier for a person to experience deindividuation, which is when a person forgets their personal views and moral compass and defers to the group. People in groups tend to forget what they know is right and wrong and follow the group instead. It can be difficult for someone who has never been caught up in groupthink to understand how this can happen, but psychologists understand that it is a real and serious problem. Deindividuation can happen offline, too. When a group begins to bully someone in a public place, it is hard for others to tell them to stop. Even people standing outside the group may feel a loss of their sense of right and wrong. It can be hard to speak up against bullies for fear of the group turning on them instead. This kind of deindividuation makes it easier for bullies to continue being cruel without punishment.

Not being able to see the person on the other side of the computer sometimes makes it easier for people to be cruel online.

The Internet also makes it easier to target people with hatred. This is when the like-minded communities become cyber mobs. Bullies will pick a target of their attacks and dehumanize the person, turning them into an enemy to be defeated. Because being in a group makes bullies feel they are right even more strongly, the Internet helps make these groups meaner. They use their anonymity, or the ability to hide their real names, as a tool for cyber abuse.

Anonymity

Some websites allow users to be anonymous. Millions of people can interact online without knowing who other people are offline. In a face-to-face conversation, each person can see the effect of their words on the other person. Without these limitations, people online often feel uninhibited by social rules about politeness. This reduces empathy for people, which can make it easier to be mean.

In a study on online behavior, the researchers noted that "anonymity can also foster a sense of impunity [freedom from consequences], loss of self-awareness, and a likelihood of acting upon normally inhibited impulses, an effect known as deindividuation."[4] Anonymity can increase the likelihood that people will form a mob mentality.

ONLINE AND OFFLINE BULLYING

"Violence online and offline ... feed into each other. Abuse may be confined to networked technologies or may be supplemented with offline harassment including vandalism, phone calls and physical assault. Similarly, the viral character of distribution is now explosive. What was once a private affair can now be instantly broadcast to billions of people across the digital world."
–United Nations Broadband Commission for Digital Development

United Nations Broadband Commission for Digital Development Working Group on Broadband and Gender, Cyber Violence Against Women and Girls: A World-Wide Wake-Up Call, 2015, www.unwomen.org/~/media/headquarters/attachments/sections/library/publications/2015/cyber_violence_gender%20report.pdf?v=1&d=20150924T154259.

In an online space where users cannot be held personally responsible for their words, many take the opportunity to be mean. After the hotly debated 2016 presidential election, Twitter finally stepped in to ban hate groups. Women and people of color had been reporting increasing threats for years on Twitter. Most of the accounts sending harassing tweets were anonymous. There were ways to block certain users but no way to make the harassment stop; members of cyber mobs simply created new Twitter profiles to harass someone. Twitter added new features that allowed users to report hateful language and targeted threats. It also worked to reduce the number of fake accounts that were used for harassment.

Many websites have restricted anonymity. To make comments on blogs or online articles, users may have to log in with their Facebook profile. This means their real name and photo will be next to any comment they make. Facebook has a policy that everyone on the website must use their real name. Some hope this will encourage people to remember that their words are permanent. Losing anonymity might stop some of the more hurtful comments.

It is easy for cyber mobs to harass people on Twitter and many other social media websites because if one of their accounts is blocked, they can quickly make another one.

Anti-masking laws exist in some states to stop anonymous harassment in person. These laws were formed to stop groups such as the Ku Klux Klan (KKK) from using masks to create anonymity. By wearing a mask, people were more likely to participate in mob mentality and forget the consequences of their actions. State laws prohibit groups of masked people from harassing others. Some people favor similar restrictions on online anonymity.

However, others believe the right to be anonymous is an important part of the Internet. The Electronic Frontier Foundation (EFF), a nonprofit organization that defends people's rights online, believes "those being harassed, as well as ... those facing domestic violence, human rights abuses, and other consequences for speaking out, can ... do so with less fear of exposure"[5] if they are allowed to remain anonymous. People who may have a good reason to remain anonymous may have to stop using the Internet if they lose that privacy.

In a 1995 Supreme Court ruling, *McIntyre v. Ohio Elections*, the court stated, "Anonymity is a shield from the tyranny of the majority."[6] The Supreme Court found that being anonymous could help everyone share opinions without being punished for unpopular ones. On the Internet, being anonymous helps people share and spread opinions that are not of the majority. These opinions may be against governments that do not protect the right to free speech. To protect the right to speak against these governments, anonymity is important.

IN DEFENSE OF ANONYMITY

"The ability to speak anonymously enables people to express minority opinions."
—Greg Norcie, technology expert

Can They Say That?

In the United States, even saying mean things about another person or group of people can be protected speech under the First Amendment to the Constitution. The First Amendment reads, "Congress shall make no law respecting an establishment of religion, or prohibiting the free exercise thereof; or abridging the freedom of speech, or of the press; or the right of the people peaceably to assemble, and to petition the government for a redress of grievances." The freedom of speech promised in the First Amendment means the U.S. government cannot stop people from speaking on a subject.

This right is important in a free society. If everyone can share their ideas and speak out about problems, then groups of people can work together to come up with solutions. Freedom of speech means everyone gets to voice their opinion, even opinions that other people may find hurtful or mean. There are some exceptions, however; threats of death or violence are not protected, and neither are libel or slander, which are lies spread to ruin a person's reputation.

Freedom of speech allows groups such as the KKK to say negative and often cruel things about certain groups, especially African Americans. The First Amendment applies to statements made online as well as offline, so the KKK is allowed to have a website that promotes its hateful views. However, the First Amendment only protects people from punishment by the government. It does not guarantee that there will be no negative consequences to a person's statements. For instance, an employer who finds out one of their employees is a KKK member can choose to fire the employee if the workplace has a policy against engaging in hate speech. People are also free to disagree with others about their views; a school may block the KKK's website or a person may write a comment online saying that they think the KKK is not a good group. Neither of these actions are a violation of the KKK's right to free speech.

In other countries, social media networks are more strictly monitored or blocked. Generally, these restrictions are put into place to prevent free speech by citizens against their government. Between June 2015 and May 2016, 24 countries restricted access to social media and other online communications. One of these countries was Uganda, which held a presidential election in 2015. The election was seen as unfair by many citizens. To restrict the ability of the Ugandan people to speak out against the election, the government closed access to social media. It reopened access only to close it down again during the president's inauguration. It did this to make it harder for protestors to organize.

The First Amendment does not mean people are protected from opposition. Counter-protests are not a violation of anyone's right to free speech.

Although freedom of speech applies both online and offline in the United States, there are still restrictions and consequences to hate speech. According to the American Bar Association, "Hate speech is speech that offends, threatens, or insults groups, based on race, color, religion, national origin, sexual orientation, disability, or other traits."[7] Hate speech is protected by the First Amendment, but "fighting words" are not. Fighting words are "those words without social value, directed to a specific individual, that would provoke a reasonable member of the group about whom the words are spoken."[8] In other words, if words spoken to a victim would make any reasonable person react with violence, these are fighting words. It can be difficult to prove whether something can be considered fighting words, and different people have different views on this. Some believe all hateful speech should be banned, while others think the term "fighting words" only refers to direct threats of violence. When people bring a case to court, the court generally weighs the evidence and decides on a case-by-case basis whether a statement falls under the category of fighting words.

Some in the United States think fighting words should no longer be an exception. They believe that since many of the words used as fighting words are said every day, they are no longer taboo. Even 20 years ago, people were shocked and offended if they heard certain swear words in public. Today, swear words have lost their shock value for many people. Some think that fighting words are the same. Since they are heard more often, the words would no longer cause a reasonable person to react in anger.

Others disagree, especially those who hear the words as an insult. Fighting words may seem to be common when people hear them a lot. However, certain words, when directed in anger at an individual, can still cause shock and a feeling of fear or pain. People who hear these fighting words as an insult might still react in anger. These include racial slurs or insults directed at a specific person. It is legal, although in poor taste, to use racial slurs in everyday conversation, but when a member of a particular race is insulted to their face with a slur, a court may find that it constitutes fighting words.

In the United States, everyone has the right to freedom of speech, and those who are victims of hate speech also have the right to speak up. Those targeted by hate speech on websites or social media can speak out against the cruel mobs and expose the authors. By reporting hate speech online, other users can act as restrictions to the spread of these ideas. Many social media platforms, such as Facebook and Twitter, try to create a balance between promoting free speech for all ideas and becoming a place for hate to spread. It is not easy to balance the two.

These conversations have taken place throughout American history. Even as early as 1798, the U.S. government tried to limit freedom of speech and freedom of the press. On July 14, 1798, Congress passed the Sedition Act. This act "permitted the prosecution of individuals who voiced or printed what the government deemed to be malicious remarks about the president or government of the United States."[9] This law was passed because some politicians feared that criticism of the government would endanger the country.

Thomas Jefferson, James Madison, and then-President John Adams were eventually able to restore freedom of speech. Since then, there have been many more attempts to stop free speech in the United States. Though freedom of speech and freedom of the press are in the Bill of Rights, U.S. citizens still must sometimes fight to maintain these rights.

Prison Time for Online Speech

In the United States, people are free to use social media for sharing ideas and supporting other people's ideas. In many other countries, though, this freedom is heavily restricted. According to a report by Freedom House, a nonprofit human rights organization, 67 percent of all Internet users live in countries that restrict speech on the Internet. In these countries, people can be punished for criticism of the government, military, or ruling family. Words may be censored or deleted online.

Free speech may even result in harsher penalties. In 38 countries, social media users were arrested because of something they posted online. In Thailand, citizens who post anything making fun of or challenging the king are faced with prison sentences. One man was faced with a 37-year prison sentence in 2015 for making fun of the king's dog online. His lawyers managed to get him released on bail—a fee people can pay for certain nonviolent crimes to avoid serving a full prison sentence—after 86 days in jail. Around the world, 27 percent of all Internet users face these types of restrictions. People around the world have been arrested for publishing, sharing, or "liking" content on Facebook.

Privacy and the Internet Age

Information that a person posts online is not always private. Many websites have settings that protect a person's privacy, but these settings are not foolproof. In one instance, a woman named Jamie took a picture of her friend Lindsey standing in front of a sign in Arlington National Cemetery, which is a military cemetery. In the picture, Lindsey is standing in front of a sign that reads "Silence and

Respect," pretending to yell and making a rude hand gesture. This was a running joke between the girls; they would take pictures of each other in front of signs, doing the opposite of what the signs said. Neither girl meant to show disrespect for the people buried in the cemetery. However, since this was an inside joke, many other people did not understand.

When Jamie put the picture on Facebook, she thought her mobile uploads were private, but she found out quickly that they were not. Someone who was not friends with her saw the picture and shared it on the Internet, and a cyber mob formed almost immediately. People who believed Lindsey was disrespecting soldiers were outraged and shared the photo in an attempt to shame her. She received so much negative attention that she could hardly leave her home for a year. She lost her job, was followed by the media, and received death and rape threats online. Other women who shared the same first and last name also suffered consequences, even though they had not done anything and did not even know Lindsey. Eventually, people lost interest and she was able to get another job, but she always lived in fear of people finding and sharing that picture again.

Some victims of cyber mobs are unable to leave their homes for a while because of all the negative attention they receive from the media.

People must be careful about what information they share because privacy laws do not protect information that people choose to make public. For instance, health information is private between doctors and their patients. However, if a patient chooses to publicly talk about their illness—for instance, by writing a blog about it—the information is no longer private.

Privacy and the Law

Some laws that are meant to protect the public can also expose private information. In June 2013, newspapers began to report about the National Security Agency (NSA) and its program on information collection. The NSA program was made possible by laws to fight terrorism. The main law, the USA PATRIOT Act (often called the Patriot Act), allowed the government to issue secret searches. It could collect information even if the person had a reasonable expectation of privacy. Personal information, such as Internet search history, website logins, and even tracking information collected by cell phones, was stored by the government. Under the Patriot Act, the government could collect this information and not tell people it was doing so. The law was challenged and slightly changed after a government employee named Edward Snowden exposed what the NSA was doing.

Another law that put public safety over privacy was Megan's Law. This law was named for Megan Kanka, who was kidnapped and murdered by a sex offender. The law states police must make information available to the public about registered sex offenders. This information includes name, photo, what crime they were convicted of, and where they live. The information could be posted online or printed on pamphlets to be given to neighbors. Some states challenged the law, saying the privacy of the sex offender was violated. Someone's name, address, photo, and criminal history are generally considered private information. Other people convicted of crimes do not have to provide this information. In the case of sex offenders, the court decided that the privacy of the sex offenders could be violated to keep children safe from perceived harm.

The Fourth Amendment to the U.S. Constitution states that people should not have their private information taken or searched without permission. This law against search and seizure protects people who are not accused of a crime from having their homes searched. Even people who have been accused of a crime cannot have their homes searched without a warrant, which a police officer can get from a judge by presenting reasons why they suspect the person of breaking the law. This also applies to electronic records. The law protects everyone from having their private information looked through.

The Fourth Amendment does not cover every person or place. A person must believe they have a reasonable expectation of privacy for a search to be illegal. One example is school lockers. Some might believe that a student should have a reasonable expectation of privacy in their locker. However, the courts have challenged this. Since lockers are school property and simply loaned to students, the school may search lockers. Students do not have a reasonable expectation of privacy because they do not own the property being searched.

On the Internet, this means electronic devices that belong to a school or company can be searched and taken away by the owner. For example, many business professionals have phones given to them by their workplace. If the workplace wants to, it can seize the phone and look through the messages. The phone is the property of the workplace, not the employee. If the employee has a personal phone, the workplace cannot search or seize that device.

Confusion About Consent

Consent is an important topic. It means giving permission for someone to do something. If someone asks if they can take a photo of someone else and the person says yes, they have given consent. On the Internet, however, consent is not as easy to define. Consent is given when a user clicks OK on the terms and conditions of a website. By saying they have read the rules, they consent to obey them. In some of these rules, the website says it wants to use information or photos posted—sometimes to sell targeted ads, other times for promotional purposes. This is a violation of privacy unless the user consents. Many people do not read these rules before they click OK, so although they are giving permission, they often do not know they have done it. Legally, however, the website is protected.

Growing Up Digital was a task force group led by the Children's Commissioner for England. The task force asked teenagers in England to read the terms and conditions of one social media website, Instagram. The teens tried to read the seven-page document. Some teens in the reading group did not finish the document because it was boring. All the teens said they did not understand the document. Members of the task force then rewrote Instagram's terms and conditions to make them easier to understand. Instead of long sentences with legal information, they created short, simple sentences. When the group of teens read the new document, many of them were upset to find out that Instagram could read their messages. The website could also sell photos posted by the teens and not give them money for it or even tell them. By agreeing to the terms and conditions and using Instagram, the teens had given away their privacy. One teen even quit the website after reading the newly worded terms and conditions.

People who do not read the terms and conditions before signing up for social media apps such as Instagram may be surprised to learn what they have allowed the app to do with their personal content.

These teens had already signed up to use Instagram. They had accepted the terms and conditions without reading or understanding them. Even adults often do not read or fully understand these documents. Without knowing it, people give away their privacy and their rights in order to use social media. Agreeing without reading a document is still consent; however, it is not informed consent. This is when someone has all the information necessary to make a good decision. The term is often used when a doctor gives a patient treatment options and lists the risks and benefits. The patient then has all the information needed to make the right decision for them. Informed consent can work on the Internet as well. Without understanding the terms of an agreement, a person cannot give informed consent. Social media websites could make the terms and conditions easier to read so everyone could give informed consent. Tumblr is one website that is committed to making sure its users fully understand the terms and conditions. Its terms of service and privacy policy are written in plain language, and under each paragraph, there is a summary of the paragraph in even plainer language, often with a funny comment to make people want to read it. For instance, one paragraph states in part, "Liking, reblogging, and replying are public actions—anyone can expand the 'notes' view on a post, for example, to see who liked, reblogged, or replied to a post. We use information about native actions to improve the Services, develop new Services, and, particularly to personalize your Tumblr experience." The summary underneath reads, "Reblogs, Likes, and Replies are a matter of public record, so if you're truly ashamed of your desires it's best to keep them to yourself. But why? Be proud of who you are. You're beautiful. We're looking you in the eyes and telling you how beautiful you are."[10]

There are consent exceptions to privacy laws. Exceptions exist about who can share their private information. Some people, under law, are not able to give consent. They cannot sign legal documents, including clicking OK on the terms and conditions of a website agreement. These people include children, people with mental disabilities, and adults who are under the influence of drugs or alcohol.

Social Networks and Hate Websites

With the launch of the first social media website in 1997 and the rise of mobile computing in the early 2000s, online spaces have become part of society. Through social media apps, groups of people can connect on any subject. Social media includes websites and apps such as Facebook, Twitter, WhatsApp, and Snapchat. They allow users to share information instantly with their groups and with the world. Many people use these websites to make friends or promote their businesses. Others use this access as a license to harass people they do not like. The Pew Research Center conducted a survey of Internet users who had experienced online harassment. Most of the harassment—66 percent—happened on social networking websites or apps.

Because people put these apps on their phones, someone who is the target of online harassment may feel like they have a bully in their pocket. Most of these apps allow someone to report a bully, who is generally called a "troll" online. The apps are supposed to treat the reports seriously. However, sometimes they do not, and one troll can become a cyber mob.

In exchange for free access to social media, these websites collect data on each user. Data collected by social media websites includes name, location, friends lists, workplace, and date of birth. If this data falls into the wrong hands, it can be used for harassment. When a cyber mob focuses on an individual, they often look online for more information about the person. Even when users of social media websites make their information private, it is easy for hackers to gain access to information. Trolls may then take this private information and use it to harass someone; for instance, they may publicly post a person's address online and encourage people to vandalize the house.

Social media can create a mob mentality very quickly. Even when social media users know each other, it can be easier to say cruel things when they are not face to face. Social media allows other users to "favorite" or "like" a post. When something cruel is said and other users show support for it, the original poster feels justified in their view. This can lead them to continue to say cruel things, thinking that if the mob agrees, it must be a true statement or something good. Some of these mean posters do not consider the feelings of their target; others get enjoyment out of hurting them.

Cyber bullies have developed a term for when they harass someone in order for others to like them. Mental health and behavior experts call this approval-seeking behavior. Online, cruel posters may say they are "doing it for the lulz." Lulz comes from the acronym for laughing out loud (LOL) and refers to trolling and other abuse done for fun. If other Internet users do not like the posts or tell the poster they are being mean, the harasser will often say they were joking or just "doing it for the lulz." People who say this believe they can do or say anything they want without consequences because their intent was just to be funny. However, their intention is not what matters. What matters is the effect a cruel or harassing post has on the victim.

Not all cyber mobs begin on social media. One website was created to share the names, home addresses, pictures, and other personal information of doctors who perform abortions in the United States. The purpose of the website was to get a mob to scare these doctors and sometimes even kill them. In a few cases, this website was the source of information for a murder. The website was eventually taken down after the owner was charged with making threats online and promoting violence.

Although that website was deleted, many others like it still exist. There is a website for white supremacists that often calls for cyber mobs. The people who run the website hate anyone who is not white or Christian. They are similar to the KKK and other hate groups. This hate website called for a "troll storm" in 2016 against Jewish people in Whitefish, Montana. The website runners were angry that the mother of a white supremacist felt she was being denied business because of her son's hate group, so they posted the names and photos of Jewish members of the town and called for trolls to harass the people listed. Acting on false information can lead people to commit crimes or target innocent people because they believe they are doing the right thing. Even if someone is actually guilty of wrongdoing, however, it is never acceptable for people to commit acts of violence or cruelty against them.

A Democracy of Harassment

Many websites and social media platforms use popularity to determine which posts are shown first. Facebook has an algorithm which learns over time what people like to see. It then shows those posts first. Reddit is a social news website where anyone with an account can post. Reddit lets users vote on what they want to see. Each post has up and down arrows next to it. Other people on the website can click to "upvote" or "downvote" something. A post with more upvotes will be shown at the top of the list of posts. In this way, only popular posts or opinions will be seen right away.

There can be problems with this type of democracy online. While anyone can vote for a post, trolls on Reddit will sometimes join together to downvote something they do not like. To prevent this from happening, Reddit created a vote-counting system that "fuzzes" the votes, meaning it changes them based on certain secret variables. Reddit employees have said the intention behind this practice is to stop people from knowing exactly how to hide posts from users they do not like.

Ellen Pao, shown here, was forced to resign as CEO of Reddit after a cyber mob formed to harass her.

Reddit members used this democratic system to try to stop anti-harassment policies from working. The users created a petition in 2015 to get the CEO of Reddit, Ellen Pao, fired after she banned five harassing sub-groups. Creating a petition is a legitimate form of protest, but the Reddit users also used trolling and harassing behavior. They created hateful photos and upvoted them to the front pages of Reddit. They also shared Pao's private information widely. In response to this treatment, Pao resigned, but she has remained vocal about eliminating online harassment.

Researchers at Stanford University conducted a study on how community feedback, such as upvotes and downvotes, changes online behavior. They found that people who write harassing comments tend to post more often when they receive negative feedback. The downvoting may make the commenter increase their level of harassment. Unlike most people, a troll might think it is fun to anger people. When they receive negative feedback, they tend to be encouraged. This has led to the popular saying, "Don't feed the trolls," meaning it is better to ignore them than try to argue with them.

A different kind of voting takes place when bullying attacks go viral. When a bullying video, post, or photo spreads to a lot of people, the bullying can get out of hand very quickly. These videos can even show up on the nightly news in many different states or countries. Just as quickly as the video goes viral, it can disappear from the public eye. However, the embarrassment and hurt can stick around.

A viral post can cause a punishment that does not fit the crime. Everyone makes mistakes they want to take back later. When a post goes viral, someone's mistakes can be spread all over the world. Instead of getting in trouble with parents or teachers, now kids can be punished by thousands of Internet comments. They may have their name permanently attached to a mistake they made. This kind of event can hurt them for life.

Is Internet Access a Human Right?

The conversation about freedom of speech has changed since the rise of online communities. Books published in one country may not have been available in another for years, so information spread more slowly. Online, one thought can be expressed instantly to the entire world. This presents many opportunities for connection and also many dangers.

The question of whether everyone has a right to be online is one that is debated often by technology groups, governments, and the public. Philosopher T.M. Scanlon wrote, "Access to means of expression is in many cases a necessary condition for participation in the political process of a country, and therefore something to which citizens have an independent right."[11] Scanlon was not talking specifically about the Internet, but rather the idea that everyone should have access to a way to speak their opinion and discuss ideas.

Governments and online communities struggle with how to keep online communities safe while not restricting this new freedom to many people. There is a balance between freedom of speech and promoting or supporting hate groups. Some countries restrict access to the Internet or what people can say online to keep people from sharing ideas. Other countries have decided that everyone has a right to be online.

The United Nations (UN), which is made up of 193 member nations, called for a special report on freedom of expression online. In 2011, the *Report of the Special Rapporteur on the Promotion and Protection of the Right to Freedom of Opinion and Expression* was published. "Unlike any other medium, the Internet enables individuals to seek, receive and impart information and ideas of all kinds instantaneously and inexpensively across national borders," Special Rapporteur Frank LaRue wrote. "By vastly expanding the capacity of individuals to enjoy their right to freedom of opinion and expression, which is an 'enabler' of other human rights, the Internet boosts economic, social and political development, and contributes to the progress of humankind as a whole."[12] While many of the UN's member nations protect their citizens' right to online access, others are still restricted or blocked.

CHAPTER 2

Harassment Types

There is no real answer to why cyber mobs attack. Each cyber mob has its own reasons for forming. Most times, the members of a cyber mob all have different reasons. However, cyber mobs do use the same types of attacks.

The Tyler Clementi Institute for CyberSafety defines three main types of harassment or bullying. The first is verbal harassment. Most of the harassment online is verbal. This includes teasing, name-calling, using inappropriate words, saying unwanted sexual things, or threatening to hurt someone.

The second kind of harassment is called social bullying. This kind of harassment means hurting someone's relationships with other people. This can be done by excluding them from groups, spreading rumors so other people exclude the person from groups, purposefully embarrassing someone in public, or telling other people to be mean to someone. This kind of bullying happens in many groups. Often, a group will exclude other people as a way to make the group members feel special and more connected.

The final type of bullying is physical. Physical bullying is when someone hits, kicks, or punches a victim. Physical bullying can also involve breaking something that someone else owns or stealing items that are important to them. This kind of bullying includes sexual assault or rape, murder, and even causing someone to commit suicide. Although someone cannot physically harm another person over the Internet, cyber mobs may make posts encouraging people to go to a victim's house and physically bully them.

Cyber mobs use a number of legal and illegal ways to gather information about a target. They may harass them both online and in person. Bullying tactics include online crimes: hacking someone's private network to steal information (theft), publishing false information about someone (libel), online stalking (criminal harassment), and speech that includes threats or name-calling (verbal harassment). Cyber harassment can even include telling the targeted person to kill themselves or other people. Mobs and individuals can use one or more of these tactics to bully someone.

Cyber mobs harass victims online and call it free speech. Some of the harassment would qualify as fighting words, but there is not generally punishment for using the words online. Users might be blocked or have their account deleted, but only if someone reports them to the website. The only words online that are taken seriously by law enforcement are called "true threats." This is when someone makes a threat to kill or otherwise hurt someone and a reasonable person would take the threat seriously. When a victim of cyber harassment feels afraid for their safety, the law has more ways to get involved.

Defining Online Abuse

The U.S. Army defines online harassment as "the use of electronic communication to inflict harm. Examples include, but are not limited to: harassment, bullying, hazing, stalking, discrimination, retaliation, or any other types of misconduct that undermine dignity and respect."[1] In an army-wide communication released in 2016, the U.S. Army chose to focus on online misconduct and its far-reaching effects. Taking steps to protect members of the army and their families from online abuse, the army reinforced its Uniform Code of Justice to support consequences for those who conduct harassment online. The army is encouraging soldiers to "Think, Type, Post ... think about the message being communicated and who could potentially view it; type a communication that is consistent with Army values; and post only those messages that demonstrate dignity and respect for self and others."[2]

1. Quoted in C. Todd Lopez, "For Those Still Unsure, Army Defines Online Misconduct," U.S. Army, August 3, 2015. www.army.mil/article/153257.
2. Quoted in Lopez, "For Those Still Unsure, Army Defines Online Misconduct."

While bullying takes place in person and online, online harassment can escalate more quickly and be harder to escape. It can be easier for anonymous bullies to target someone in all parts of their life. Cyber mobs may form on one social media platform but can transition to other platforms. For instance, people may start harassing someone through Twitter and eventually move to Facebook and Instagram as well. Through these platforms, bullies can find where the target works and may create false or mean posts on business websites such as Yelp or even the website of the victim's company. People's connected lives can provide cyber mobs with easy access to their personal and professional lives.

Trolls and Trolling

In face-to-face communication, people learn to read social cues such as facial expression, body language, or eye movement. These cues help people understand how someone else feels. For instance, if the person they are talking to does not make eye contact, it may be clear they are uncomfortable. This helps people understand that they should ask questions or change the subject. On the Internet, people cannot see these social cues. Since most things on the Internet are expressed in words alone, they also miss out on tone of voice. One person may read a post as a joke, while another person may see the same post as serious.

Body language and facial expression are important indicators of what a person is feeling. When people interact through the Internet and cannot see these, they may find it easier to ignore someone else's feelings.

On the Internet, people may lose their sense of reality. They may believe that being online frees them from consequences. Without social cues, trolls may lose the inhibition that comes from seeing someone face to face. Inhibitions keep people from doing harmful or dangerous things. It is an unconscious feeling that they should not do something. Inhibitions may stop someone from saying something mean. Offline, trolls might be concerned with what others think. They might be able to read social cues and participate in society in appropriate ways.

Researchers believe trolls think too much about themselves. They may want to attract attention and do not care if the attention is negative. Trolls may give their target a set of made up qualities. Instead of knowing someone as a person, a troll may see a person as an obstacle. They might tell themselves a target is more powerful or dangerous than they really are. Trolls tend to believe the Internet is a game they have to win. Winning happens by outsmarting other people and "destroying" them with words and images.

Trolls want to feel more powerful or better than others. They may lie about who they are; for example, they may make up stories about how they are rich and famous or popular. In reality, many trolls are people who have been bullied themselves. They are often left out of groups, so they go online to make themselves feel accepted. Trolls may also take out their anger about problems in their life on people online. Because they lose their inhibitions, trolls feel they can say whatever they want.

Studies of trolls have found that many of them enjoy making other people suffer. They find it fun to cause other people harm. This is called sadistic or psychopathic behavior. The worst trolls feel no remorse or guilt for hurting other people. Wanting to hurt other people is not normal; psychologists call it anti-social behavior. When a group of people who do not care about the feelings of others get together, they will hurt other people just to impress members of the cyber mob. This status-seeking is similar to attention-seeking behavior.

Cyber mobs often form online around trolling behavior. Trolling starts most often with a reaction to an idea or comment shared online. Researchers into online behavior define trolling as "posting (of) incendiary comments with the intent of provoking others into conflict."[13] Trolls say mean things and hurt other people so the victim will react. Trolls will then try to get other people to feel sorry for them so many people will post cruel things to the victim. They often trick other people into becoming a cyber mob.

Gabriella Coleman, an expert on Internet abuse, described trolling behavior as "a combination of four things: pranking, trickery, deceit and defilement."[14] A group of trolls can quickly become a cyber mob when they find support online. Cyber mobs and trolls may harass victims for ideas that are different. However, an individual troll may start provoking someone online for no good reason. Trolls often choose to mock personal characteristics of a target. These include race, ethnicity, gender, and sexuality. Women, especially women of color, are a favorite target of trolling behavior. Trolls may make crude comments about a person's body, claim a target has a sexually transmitted disease, or state someone has sex with many people. Their goal is to get other people angry enough to become a cyber mob.

Becoming the target of a cyber mob is distressing and overwhelming. The victim often receives dozens—sometimes even hundreds—of upsetting messages.

Trolling has caused restrictions of online speech for everyone. Instead of writing thoughtful comments for or against an online article, trolls use threatening language and abusive comments. They often focus on the personal characteristics of the writer instead of the merits of an online argument. In this way, trolls make hateful speech personal. For instance, in 2012, a writer for the University at Buffalo's student newspaper, the *Spectrum*, wrote an opinion piece about why people should not get tattoos. In the physical copy of the newspaper, it was published next to a pro-tattoo article, but online, it appeared on its own. Many of the things Lisa Khoury, the author of the article, said about people who choose to get tattoos were offensive and inaccurate. For example, she implied that women who get tattoos have no morals and are not happy with the body they were born with. Her comments made many people angry, but instead of arguing with her point of view, they attacked her as a person. She received death threats, e-mails, and Facebook posts telling her she was ugly, as well as other upsetting messages. Many of these people were not normally trolls; they were regular people with tattoos who got angry enough to lose their inhibitions and say things they probably would not have said to Khoury's face. Although Khoury's original comments were not kind to people with tattoos, she did not deserve to be personally attacked by a cyber mob. The experience left her upset for several weeks.

STAY CALM AND KIND

"It's valuable to allow all sides of an argument to be heard. But it's not valuable for there to be personal attacks, or to have messages with an extremely angry tone. Even someone who is making a legitimate point but with an angry tone is hurting the nature of the argument, because they are promoting people to respond in kind."
–Art Markman, professor of psychology at the University of Texas at Austin

Quoted in Natalie Wolchover, "Why Is Everyone on the Internet So Angry?," Scientific American, July 25, 2012. www.scientificamerican.com/article/why-is-everyone-on-the-internet-so-angry/

Bullying with Memes and Videos

Pictures and videos may be taken without someone's knowledge and posted online without their permission. Other times, they are put on the Internet by the people in them and then used for hurtful purposes by others. Once information is posted on the Internet, the person who posted it no longer has any control over its use. Every photo uploaded to a website or an app is available for other people to find and use. For example, many memes are created using personal photos. Sometimes, these memes are real photos of people who often do not know their photo is being used.

Memes and other pictures of real people are often used in a joking fashion by people online. These jokes can become cruel quickly and can spread throughout the Internet. Trolls and other cyber mob participants do not see the real pain caused by cruel memes. Victims of these meme campaigns often find out about the use of their pictures much later. Because the picture has been shared so many times, it can be difficult to find out who is responsible. Since the picture is often in many places, it can be impossible to have it removed from the Internet. Victims of bullying through memes are often affected offline as well.

One of the first accounts of cyberbullying using a meme or video was of a 15-year-old Canadian boy named Ghyslain Raza. Raza recorded a video of himself performing Star Wars moves. The video was intended to be private, but some of his classmates found it and shared it online. Raza became known as "Star Wars Kid," and although there was nothing wrong with what he was doing in the video, a cyber mob formed to share the video across the Internet in an effort to shame Raza for his interest in Star Wars. Many people even suggested that he should commit suicide. The video was used to bully Raza both online and at his school. Eventually, the bullying became so bad that he quit school and had to seek psychiatric help. Fortunately, he went on to become a lawyer and now helps raise awareness about cyberbullying. Other stories do not always end so happily. It is easy for people to tell others to just ignore people's hurtful words, but being told over and over again to commit suicide has a strong mental impact on people, and some eventually do kill themselves.

Hacking: Breaking and Entering

To harass people online, individual members of a cyber mob may use hacking to gain more information or access to a person's Internet accounts. Hacking is defined as interrupting or changing the normal network connections. A network is how computers connect to the Internet. When hackers get into the connection, they can steal information. Hackers can gain access to things such as the login and password to accounts, health records, school records, and even banking websites.

Once a hacker has stolen login information, they have as much access to people's accounts as the owner of the account. Using this information, a hacker can change someone's password, locking them out. Then they can pretend to be the person and post content they would not normally say. No one looking at the websites would know it was not the person whose name is on the website, and it is difficult to prove that someone else has posted on their behalf. This can cause embarrassing or hurtful things to be said in someone's name. Again, the goal is to get others so angry that they lose their inhibitions and join together to become a cyber mob.

Trolls may hack into someone's personal accounts to steal their financial information or private photos and messages.

Hackers may also use stolen information to ruin someone's finances. By stealing credit card or Social Security numbers, they can make purchases in someone else's name. There are ways the person can prove they did not make the charges, but often, this is a difficult and time-consuming process, and it may take quite a while to get their money back. Keeping personal information private is important for protection both online and offline. Cyberbullies will often use stolen information to copy photos or personal texts and e-mails. They may try to use this information to embarrass the victim. Everyone says things in private they might not want other people to know. By hacking into an e-mail account, the cyberbullies can find e-mails and photos that a victim might not want other people to see. The bullies can then spread these private documents online to make others want to target the victim.

Another way trolls who steal password information hurt victims is by deleting information, such as the victim's social media accounts. Many people use social media to connect with friends or other support systems. By deleting these accounts, the victim may lose contact with supportive people. This can isolate a victim and make them feel alone in the world, which negatively affects their mental state and makes them more likely to be hurt emotionally by the things the cyber mob is saying.

Sometimes, cyber bullies do not need to use computer or network hacking to steal information. They may get a cyber mob started to harass the victim until they release private information. These trolls manipulate, or control forcefully, to get what they want. The victim might release information under all this pressure and then feel guilty. They might not report manipulation because they feel they gave in to bullies, even though it is not their fault.

Doxing: Releasing Private Information

Once they gain access to personal information such as a home address or phone number, cyber mobs will typically intensify their attacks. Trolls may publish the personal information of a target. This unauthorized sharing of private information is called doxing. (The word "dox" comes from an abbreviation for "document.") Some doxed information may be easy to find. This could include Facebook photos or an e-mail address. Other information could be a Social Security number, an address, or other private information that generally requires hacking to find.

Doxing is done to make a victim scared enough to stop doing something. Sometimes, a troll will respond to an argument on the Internet with the home address of someone they want to silence. The post often includes a threat. Doxing is a personal crime; it is an attack on a specific person to get them to be quiet about their ideas or to feel fear.

During the 2016 U.S. presidential election, TV personality Lou Dobbs accidentally doxed a woman who had accused

Donald Trump, the Republican nominee for president, of sexual harassment. On Twitter, Dobbs retweeted a photo of the woman's phone number and address and expressed support for Trump. Twitter's terms of service state that users cannot post the private information of other people, including home addresses. However, all Twitter can do as a result is take down the post and ban the user. There is nothing stopping users from posting that information and sharing it widely before Twitter is made aware. Though Dobbs apologized, the tweet had already been widely shared and photos or screenshots had already been taken before he could delete the tweet. Fortunately, the woman did not report anyone taking advantage of the situation.

Sharing someone's phone number online may cause that person to receive many threatening phone calls from people they do not know. Even if they do not answer the calls, simply receiving them can be frightening.

Although Dobbs did not dox the woman on purpose, the consequences for the victim could have been drastic. Trolls who dox someone often use the excuse that they did not do anything. They say they just released information; it was other people who performed the harassment. These doxers do not take responsibility for the fear and pain their actions cause.

Doxing is often seen by other members of the cyber mob as permission to use this personal contact information to continue harassing the target. Doxers feel as though their victim deserves it. In one case, a woman named Laura paid for someone else to write a college paper for her. The man wrote the paper but also wrote a blog post about it, listing her full name and the college she went to. He said he was going to turn her in to the college dean after she submitted her paper. Many people who read the blog post became angry at Laura for cheating and turned it into a personal issue. They made judgments about her personality they had no way of knowing, such as that she was rich and spoiled and had never had to do any work for herself. This may not have been true, but people convinced themselves it was so they would feel their harassment of her was justified. Some people who read the blog post used the information the man had shared to find her phone number and call her. They told her they knew what she did and threatened to tell everyone. Other members of this cyber mob started e-mailing the college. Their goal was to get Laura expelled from school as punishment for buying a paper. She contacted the blog writer and asked him to remove her last name. He did, but it was too late. Laura and her family continued to be harassed. Even years later, the information comes up when her name is searched.

When Online Comes Home

Trolls will sometimes stalk people, both online and offline. Stalkers become obsessed with their victim. They often try to control the target. The stalker will try to follow the target and find out where they are at all times. They might also try to get the victim alone by spreading rumors to friends and family that make them think the victim wants to be alone or is too mean to hang out with anymore.

Cyberstalking is using technology to harass someone repeatedly. This can include sending a lot of e-mails or text messages, going to multiple websites to post about someone in a mean way, and spreading rumors online. Some cyberstalkers will create new websites just to say cruel things about their victim. They may use a tactic called Google bombing, which is when a person makes all of the bad or untrue posts about a target show up first in a Google search. They can do this by hyperlinking all the posts across different websites. When Google or another search engine looks for information, the first results it displays are the ones that show up the most. Many cyberstalkers try to start a cyber mob by making false accusations about a victim and asking other people to help shame or punish them. These accusations could be that the victim has committed a crime such as child abuse or that the victim is the one saying mean things about other people.

Cyberstalking can be difficult for people to identify, so people may sometimes do things without realizing their actions have legal consequences. In one case, two twelve-year-old girls were charged with cyberstalking when they hacked into a third girl's Facebook page and posted pictures of the victim. The girls had Photoshopped their victim's pictures so she appeared to have horns on her head and to be holding knives. They e-mailed other people from the girl's account asking for sexual favors. All three of the girls had been friends at school. The cyberstalkers were caught and sentenced to community service.

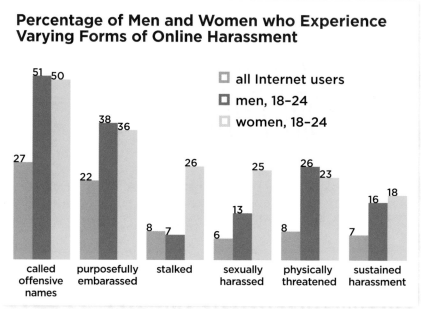

Percentage of Men and Women who Experience Varying Forms of Online Harassment

Although both men and women experience cyberbullying, their experiences tend to be different, as this information from the Pew Research Center shows. Men are more likely to be called names, while women are much more likely to be stalked.

Cyberstalkers can be men or women, and sometimes, they make true threats that the police treat seriously. There is no legal test to determine whether something is a true threat, so police look at the context. They will take into account things such as whether the two people know each other, whether the target seemed scared by the threat, and whether the person making the threat has a history of violence.

True threats are often graphic. They may include specific details such as how and when a person or their family will be hurt or killed. True threats might mention where the person lives and how they are being watched. Law enforcement takes true threats seriously. Under the Violence Against Women Act of 2000 in the United States, cyberstalking is a federal crime.

The first case of cyberstalking to result in death and go to trial involved a divorced couple. Christine Belford divorced her husband David Matusiewicz and was seeking custody of their three children. Matusiewicz used cyberstalking and other trolling behavior to try to stop her from gaining custody. He and his parents and sister formed a cyber mob. They posted fake stories on the Internet that Belford was abusing the children. They hacked into her Facebook account and used it to write horrible things. They would send messages to the court and child protective services against Belford.

Belford told police and her lawyers about the cyberstalking and abuse. The cyber mob continued to harass her. It expanded to include other people in her community. These people believed the lies Matusiewicz and his relatives had posted, so they became angry enough to harass Belford, feeling that she deserved it. A court hearing was scheduled in 2013 to settle the cyberstalking charges. At the courthouse, her former father-in-law shot and killed Belford and her friend Laura Beth Mulford. Belford's ex-husband and family were convicted of cyberstalking and murder.

Calling All Cars: Swatting

Another tactic cyber mobs use to scare and threaten people offline is called swatting. This is when someone makes a call to the target's local police and tells them a crime is being committed. Swatters typically state that a murder or hostage situation is taking place to draw a large police response. This motivates police to move quickly and to bring their Special Weapons and Tactics, or SWAT, teams. These teams use heavily armored vehicles and high-powered weapons to respond to crime. When there is no crime being committed, the arrival of SWAT teams can lead to frightening consequences for the target, including accidental death.

A 17-year-old boy in Canada used the power of American SWAT teams to frighten and harass other members of his video game community. Over the course of a few years, the boy called in many swatting events all across the United States. "This kid was unbelievable," said the detective who tracked him down. "He was calling everyone and everything—schools, businesses, private residences, law enforcement, the FBI's weapons of mass destruction hotline, even Disneyland."[15] The swatter was eventually caught after swatting two homes in Ohio and live-streaming them online. He was charged in Canada with 23 counts of extortion, public mischief, and criminal harassment.

Swatting is a terrifying experience for victims because SWAT teams are trained to respond with force to violent criminals. Innocent people can be hurt when the SWAT team has been led to believe they are a threat.

For the victim of swatting, the fear of another attack can linger for years. This fear can cause post-traumatic stress disorder (PTSD), which is a psychological condition that occurs after a frightening event. This disorder is commonly associated with soldiers, but researchers and doctors have recently found that people who experience any traumatic event may develop PTSD. These events range from childhood abuse to rape to being the victim of a vicious cyber mob. The effects of this psychological damage can last through adulthood, especially if the victim does not seek therapy. People suffering from PTSD tend to avoid things that remind them of the experiences that caused the condition. Often, they do not wish to talk about or even think about these events. They may begin avoiding family, friends, and activities that they once enjoyed. They may also have nightmares or flashbacks, which are vivid memories of the traumatic event.

Victims of swatting and doxing often continue to live in fear of the cyber mob even after the mob stops harassing them. Some change homes or workplaces so a cyber mob will lose access to their real location. This may give the victim some peace, but it can also cause problems for others. In one situation, a family in Georgia was the target of two swatting calls. The police officer who was in charge of the investigation believed the calls were made because someone who was active in online gaming used to live at that address. He believed the people responsible for the swatting attacks did not know the gamer had moved.

Many victims feel the only way to stop a cyber mob is to stop using the Internet and go into hiding. Lenny Pozner is the father of a child who was killed in the Sandy Hook Elementary shooting in 2012. Trolls began to spread rumors online that the Sandy Hook shooting had been faked, and a cyber mob started to harass the parents of the children killed. Pozner has been targeted by this cyber mob for many years. One woman was arrested for making a true threat against him on the Internet. Pozner moved away from Sandy Hook and frequently moves to protect his address. He lives in fear of the cyber mob committing real violence, but this has not stopped him from fighting back by creating the HONR Network. This organization connects families who have lost loved ones in violent incidents so they can support each other and fight back against people who falsely accuse these families of lying about the circumstances of their loved ones' deaths.

CHAPTER 3

Consequences of Cyber Attacks

The actions of cyber mobs can have devastating consequences for their victims. Targets can lose jobs and job opportunities, their reputation, and even their lives. Stolen information that is posted on the Internet, including addresses and other personal information, can be difficult to remove.

Victims of cyber mobs can lose relationships as a result of the abuse and begin to feel very alone. Cyber mobs may exclude a victim from social situations or block them online. With children and teenagers, most cyberbullying comes from other kids they know at school. Like bullying offline, cyberbullying can affect friendships. Friends who know the victim in real life may distance themselves because they do not want to become victims of the cyber mob, too. At school, this can isolate a victim and make them feel even more alone. Victims of cyberbullying lose trust in the people around them who do not help them fight against the cyber mob.

Family members who have experienced doxing or swatting may fear having the victim of a cyber mob living in the family home. A victim may be asked to move away from parents or children to protect other family members from harm. Even if none of these things happen, the victim can still suffer psychological consequences such as depression, anxiety, or PTSD.

Loss at Work and School

Many schools provide information to students and teachers about bullying and cyberbullying. People are more aware of the issue than ever before. However, 34 percent of the students surveyed by the Cyberbullying Research Center said they had been bullied. More than half of the students reported that the cyberbullying affected their ability to feel safe at school.

At one middle school in Connecticut, an anonymous student created a Facebook page called Let's Start Drama and encouraged other students to send gossip or rumors. The owner of the page, who earned the nickname "Drama Queen" from writer Emily Bazelon, then spread the gossip and encouraged bullying at school. More than 500 local teenagers were actively spreading rumors and bullying other kids through the page. The conflict continued in school, with some students getting into physical fights over things that had been posted on the page. A school official reported it to Facebook twice, hoping the website would disable it. Although the page broke Facebook's terms of service in several different ways, including the fact that Drama Queen was using a fake e-mail account and that the page promoted bullying, the page stayed up until Bazelon, who wrote about the story for *The Atlantic*, went to Facebook headquarters to see why. The reporter found that the people on Facebook's Hate and Harassment Team had to deal with so many requests each day that sometimes they made mistakes and left up a page that should have been taken down. Let's Start Drama was deleted by Facebook after the reporter showed it to the Hate and Harassment Team, but this shows that users cannot always count on Facebook or other social media websites to help them fight cyber mobs.

Cyberbullying can have severe effects for victims. They may have trouble concentrating in school and begin to suffer psychological problems, such as depression and anxiety. These effects can stay with a person into adulthood. If the information is not deleted, it will always be available for a person to look at online. This includes future friends, employers, and partners of the victim of bullying.

Fortunately, cyberbullying can have consequences for the bullies as well. This was true for a lawyer named Anthony Ciolli. In 2005, when he was a law student, Ciolli was a director of a website called AutoAdmit. This website contained message boards with numerous posts against African Americans, Jewish people, and women. Ciolli and Jarrett Cohen, another owner of the website, did not censor or remove the hateful messages because they believed they should be left up due to freedom of speech. These hateful messages went on for years. In 2007, Ciolli lost a job offer from a law firm when the *Washington Post* published an article about the website's hateful

Cecil the Lion

A Minnesota dentist named Walter Palmer was the victim of a cyber mob in 2015, after he went on a hunt organized by a group in the African country of Zimbabwe. He shot a lion just outside of a national park. The lion was named Cecil and had been a mascot of the park. Posts began to pop up on social media saying that Palmer had committed a crime, although the hunt was organized legally through the company. They were also angry that he had killed an animal just to take its head home as a trophy.

A cyber mob began to call for people to harass Palmer. Many people started calling his dental office and leaving threatening messages. His website became a place where trolls posted false bad reviews of his dentistry. Many people called for him to lose his practice completely; they felt he deserved to lose everything. This shows how out of proportion a cyber mob's response can be. Palmer had not committed any crime; people may have disagreed with his choice to hunt a lion for sport, but he did not do so illegally. People often do things other people may disagree with. However, most people are not punished as severely for this as the victims of cyber mobs are.

Protests erupted both online and offline when Walter Palmer killed Cecil.

posts. The law firm said Ciolli's behavior was unacceptable and the company did not want anyone to think it approved of his actions.

Cyber mobs will often target a person at work. Members of the mob will send hateful messages to a boss or coworkers of the victim. Many times, a cyber mob will tell the employer that the victim should be lose their job. In some cases, the employer agrees, and the victim is fired.

Emotional Distress

Bullying and cyber attacks can cause long lasting emotional problems for victims. Some victims of cyber mobs turn to alcohol or drug abuse. Many develop depression and anxiety. Victims with depression might stay in bed and miss school or work. Some victims develop anger problems or try to go out of their way to be nice to everyone to prevent further bullying.

Victims of cyber mobs feel real fear from the cruel words they see on the screen. "Psychiatric injury, however, is but one possible harmful result of being mobbed," wrote Dr. Kenneth Westhues, a professor who studies mob behavior. "Some mobbing targets keep their sanity but succumb to cardiovascular disease—hypertension [high blood pressure], heart attack, or stroke. Most suffer loss of income and reputation. Marital breakdown and isolation from friends and family are also common outcomes."[16]

Bystander PTSD

Seeing so much hate online can cause PTSD symptoms even in people who are not the target of a cyber mob. According to a study by the Pew Research Center, 73 percent of people said they had witnessed someone else being bullied online. Being reminded of the cruelty people are capable of can make people feel fearful without being the direct target of these words, especially if the statements could be applied to them as well. For instance, a woman who sees anti-woman messages directed at a different woman may still feel upset. Researchers and community activists who study online abuse can be affected as well. While it is a good idea to think about things before posting them online, witnessing a cyber mob attack may make people afraid to post even harmless messages.

Shaming and Reputation Damage

Cyber mobs often cause damage to someone's reputation, which is the shared ideas about a person based on outside information. When people hear and believe negative rumors, they form a negative opinion of the person they are hearing these statements about. Making such statements is called defamation of character. Defamation does not involve simply insulting someone, especially if the insult is an opinion. To count as defamation, the statement must have four qualities, according to Nolo, a website that aims to make difficult legal concepts easier for the average person to understand. Someone who is trying to prove defamation of character must be able to show that the statement was:

- **Published:** The statement was written down (libel) where other people could see it or spoken (slander) where other people could hear it.

- **False:** The statement must be able to be proven false with concrete evidence, otherwise the statement is not considered to be damaging. For example, saying that someone robbed a bank when they did not is something that can be proven false by an investigation.

- **Injurious:** The statement must be damaging to the person's reputation. The person must be able to prove that they suffered in some way from the statement, such as being fired from a job or expelled from school.

- **Unprivileged:** In certain rare circumstances, people's right to free speech is protected even when they defame someone. This generally only applies to lawmakers and people who testify in court.

Defamation can have serious consequences for the target. Reputation is how people and groups decide someone is trustworthy. Ruining a person's reputation can cause them to lose friends, job opportunities, scholarships, and more. To help people protect themselves, the Supreme Court has ruled that people can sue others for defamation, or take them to court to clear their name and hold the other person accountable for their actions. The Court said reputation law protects "the essential dignity and worth of every human being—a concept at the root of any decent system of ordered liberty."[17]

When an anonymous woman accused Kobe Bryant (shown here) of sexual assault in 2003, a cyber mob harassed a woman they mistakenly believed had made the report.

Cyber mobs often defame their targets. Sometimes, this is on purpose, but other times, people spread a rumor believing it is true, then find out it is false. Whether they do it on purpose or by accident, the consequences are the same for the victim, which is why people should always do their own research before sharing something negative.

Sometimes innocent bystanders are victimized by cyber mobs. In one case, a young woman accused basketball player Kobe Bryant of sexual assault in 2003, and some people believed she was lying. News reports of the rape accusation had not released the woman's name, but they did talk about the town she lived in and the school she went to. Internet commenters tried to find out for themselves who the woman was. They decided it was a young woman named Katie Lovell. In fact, Lovell had nothing to do with the incident. The only connection was that she went to high school with the accuser. However, people started writing hateful things about Lovell on the Internet. Someone released her photo online without her permission. Lovell tried to tell people they had accused the wrong person, but few believed her. The experience of seeing so many nasty posts about her online was extremely upsetting for Lovell, even though she knew the posts were not true.

Other victims have actually done something society sees as wrong, and cyber mobs form as a way of shaming them. Shaming happens in groups as a way to keep the social norms, or unwritten rules of society. Online shaming can sometimes seem like a normal or funny thing. For example, some men who sit on public transportation take up a lot of room by sitting with their legs spread open, pushing into other people's seating areas. When someone sees a man do this in public, they might take his picture, share it online, and complain about how the man is taking up too much space. They do this to try to enforce the social norm of not invading other people's personal space. The man whose picture was shared may never find out, but this kind of shaming works for anyone who sees it. By seeing the anonymous man be shamed, others understand that the punishment for breaking this social norm might be that others laugh at them online. This kind of fear often makes people keep social norms in place. However, when a cyber mob forms, the shaming is generally far harsher than it should be. Trolls and cyber mobs violate social norms online by being cruel, but they feel it is okay because they have convinced themselves their target deserves it.

Bullycide

Suicide can be one tragic result of a cyber mob attack. Often, cyber mobs will encourage a victim to commit suicide. Hearing this message multiple times from multiple people—even strangers who do not know anything about them—can lead a victim to commit or attempt suicide to escape the abuse.

Some activists have started calling suicide caused by bullying "bullycide." Brandy Vela was one victim of bullycide. Vela was a senior in high school when she took her own life after years of bullying, both online and offline. She had been harassed about her weight for years at school. By 2016, the harassment had moved online. Bullies created a fake Facebook profile for her and used the account to send sexual messages to other people. They even posted her real telephone number so men would call about the sexual offers. Other trolls would call or text late at night. They talked about her weight and about her physical features. Every time Vela reported a cyberbullying page, Facebook would take it down. Within days, another one would be started. Vela was never able to find out who

Amanda Todd and Anonymous

Sometimes, cyber mobs form to try to help people. In one instance, a young woman in Canada named Amanda Todd posted a video to YouTube shortly before her suicide. In it, she explained that she had been harassed by an unknown man for years online. The man had repeatedly used a photo of Todd's breasts to intimidate her and to shame her by showing it to her friends and classmates. After her death, the "hacktivist" group Anonymous created a cyber mob to find the identity of the man. Anonymous is a loosely connected group of people on the Internet who claim to expose secrets for the greater good of society. Within a few days, they had identified the man and shared his name online. The response to Anonymous's actions was mixed. Some people were happy the man had been identified so he could be brought to justice, but others felt that sharing his identity online would open the door to the creation of a cyber mob to harass him, especially since Anonymous's information could not be used as proof of the man's actions in a court case against him. If someone does something wrong to another person, do they deserve the same treatment in return? This is a moral question that has been debated for centuries, and it is unlikely that everyone will ever come to the an agreement on it.

Anonymous is a loosely organized group of hackers that comes together as a cyber mob for certain causes. It opposes terrorism, police brutality, cyberbullying, and other forms of harassment. In public, Anonymous members sometimes disguise themselves by wearing the style of mask made popular in the movie V for Vendetta.

was behind the fake profiles. However, in March 2017, four months after she killed herself, two suspects were arrested: Vela's ex-boyfriend, 21-year-old Andres Arturo Villagomez, and his girlfriend, 22-year-old Karinthya Sanchez Romero. The investigation is ongoing as of June 2017.

Human Rights Violations

Universal human rights include not only access to the Internet, but being able to participate online without fear of discrimination. When cyber mobs or trolls use slurs, taboo words, and threatening language, they are abusing the human rights of a victim. Civil rights in the United States include freedom of speech and assembly. In the modern age, this can include being able to log on to the Internet and talk to other people. Victims of cyber mobs are often pushed out of online spaces. This violates their right to free assembly.

Many victims of cyber mobs will take a break from being online. Some will even leave the Internet permanently. Some victims, though, feel they cannot leave the Internet because they need to stand up for themselves and correct the false information being spread by the cyber mob. There is no right or wrong way to handle being a victim of lies online. Sometimes, correcting the cyber mob will make the harassment worse. Other times, victims feel more fear about leaving the conversation.

Another human right online, as defined by the Council of Europe, is the right to privacy. When a cyber mob steals and publishes personal information, it is violating human rights. Invading privacy and taking someone's information is theft. The theft of privacy is covered under laws and universal rights.

Changing the Internet for the Worse

Some trolls and cyber mobs may use denial of service to stop victims from using the Internet. A denial of service attack, sometimes abbreviated as DoS, is when the connection to the Internet is blocked. The victim may think it is a problem with their computer or even call their Internet service provider (ISP) to see what is wrong, but if the attack is caused by a troll, there may be nothing the ISP can do to fix it.

A New Twist on an Old Practice

In his book *So You've Been Publicly Shamed*, author Jon Ronson explained that public shaming makes people feel powerful. Until the 1830s, punishments in the United Kingdom and United States were held in the town square. People would be whipped or put in the stocks, and the general public would be invited to watch, laugh, and sometimes throw things at the person being punished. With the rise of the Internet, individuals once again have a public voice. Some may feel it is their duty to shame someone because they believe that when they do this, they are making the world a better place by stopping someone else from doing the same thing. Others may shame people in an effort to divert attention from their own mistakes.

Because of the dehumanizing effect of the Internet, people are much harsher when they publicly shame people online than they would be if someone they knew had made the same mistake. In one example, Ronson talked about a journalist named Jonah Lehrer who had written a book about musician Bob Dylan. Lehrer had made small changes to several of Dylan's quotes, and when he was exposed, he faced a lot of criticism. When he made a public apology, many people refused to accept it; they posted on Twitter that he did not seem like he was truly sorry and that he should never have done it in the first place. In cyber mob cases such as this one, a mob is often much more eager to publicly shame someone than they are to forgive them.

In the past, stocks were devices used to imprison someone in the town square so they could be publicly shamed.

When victims of cyber mobs leave the Internet, they lose the ability to participate in the world. They may lose touch with world events, lose job opportunities, or lose money if their job involves a lot of online work. Additionally, if a person fears being a target of a cyber mob, they may not speak their true feelings. In 1919, former U.S. Supreme Court Justice Oliver Wendell Holmes said about ideas that "the best test of truth is the power of the thought to get itself accepted in the competition of the market."[18] A conversation about ideas cannot happen when people are scared. When only one idea is presented, it may be accepted as the truth. This censorship of ideas hurts everyone.

When ideas or beliefs are challenged by the opposing side, people are able to make arguments for what they believe in. This causes them to really think about why they believe something. Thinking strengthens an argument. Without having to think about an idea, people may believe something and not know why. They may also believe false things because they have never had to think about whether their belief is true or false. When voices are silenced by cyber mobs, the debate stops, and the truth can be hidden.

CHAPTER 4

Special Issues with Protected Groups

When a person or group of people say cruel things about another group of people based on their gender, race, ethnicity, religion, sexual orientation, or physical and mental abilities, this can be termed hate speech. Hate speech is using words or images to scare, silence, or otherwise harm a person in one of these protected groups.

In other countries, hate speech is banned or more restricted. In Germany, symbols of anti-Semitism—hatred of Jewish people—are banned. It is illegal for people to deny the Holocaust or use Nazi words and images to hurt Jewish people. In the United Kingdom (UK), a law called the Public Order Act 1986 forbids people from using hate speech. It bans threatening, abusive, or insulting behavior in regard to someone's race. Many other countries have bans on speech that is used to start violence against protected groups.

For protected groups, the Internet can sometimes become a scary place. Hate speech online can turn into real life hate crimes. Even if violence does not happen, being the target of a cyber mob can cause pain and fear. People in protected groups are often harassed in real life as well as online. Every time they are harassed, the fear and pain get worse.

Minority Groups on the Internet

The most frequent targets of harassment are women, members of the LGBT+ community, people with disabilities or special needs, religious minorities, and people of color. Many times, victims of cyber mobs fall into more than one of these categories. According to a 2016 survey by social justice organization Rad Campaign on online harassment, the majority of abuse—63 percent—takes place on Facebook, but people also reported harassment through e-mail, Twitter, YouTube, Snapchat, Tumblr, and more.

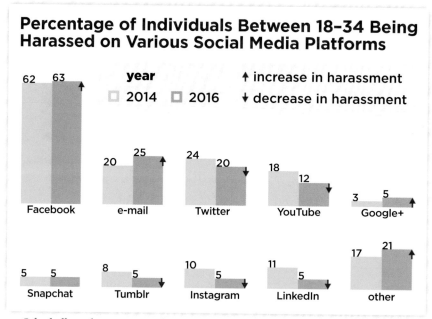

Percentage of Individuals Between 18–34 Being Harassed on Various Social Media Platforms

year — ☐ 2014 ☐ 2016

↑ increase in harassment
↓ decrease in harassment

	2014	2016
Facebook	62	63 ↑
e-mail	20	25 ↑
Twitter	24	20 ↓
YouTube	18	12 ↓
Google+	3	5 ↑
Snapchat	5	5
Tumblr	8	5 ↓
Instagram	10	5 ↓
LinkedIn	11	5 ↓
other	17	21 ↑

Cyberbullying happens most frequently on Facebook, but it can happen anywhere people interact online, as this information from Rad Campaign shows.

Anyone can become the victim of cyberbullying. Throughout the eight years that President Barack Obama and First Lady Michelle Obama were in the White House, they were often targets of online abuse. Cyberbullies would alter photos of Michelle Obama and call her names. In 2016, a woman in West Virginia named Pamela Ramsey Taylor tweeted racist comments about the First Lady. She was fired from her job at a nonprofit organization soon afterward; her employer never stated that the tweet was the reason she was fired, but the state government requested assurance that the company was following anti-discrimination policies. Government officials were concerned that Taylor's racist views would affect the quality of the help she gave any black families through the nonprofit organization.

A more sinister cyber mob appeared at the University of Pennsylvania in November 2016. African American freshmen were invited to a new online group. When they joined, they discovered that it was full of hateful posts and taboo language. The posts said that violent acts would be carried out on campus against African

American students. The group set up dates and times to lynch, or hang, each student. The university quickly responded and shut down the website, but not before many of the freshmen had experienced emotional harm and fear for their safety on campus.

Women of color who use Twitter report being harassed daily. Imani Gandy, a black woman who often tweets about racial injustice, reported abuse to Twitter for two years. The troll who was targeting her created hundreds of Twitter accounts, which he used to send racist tweets to Gandy. Racist threats are against the rules on Twitter, but the website could not keep up with all the accounts the troll was creating. He also harassed anyone who talked to Gandy on Twitter.

Women and the Internet

According to the Pew Research Center, women and men log on to the Internet in equal numbers in the United States, but women are more likely to be stalked and harassed on the Internet by both individuals and cyber mobs. The organization Working to Halt Online Abuse (WHOA) reported that between 2000 and 2011, more than 72 percent of reported harassment online was targeted at women. Abuse that starts with individual cyberbullies may turn into a cyber mob. Some spaces online, such as gaming and sports websites, often host more male users than female. When women participate more in these spaces, cyber mobs may form to bully them away.

Women who work online, such as bloggers and journalists, get a lot of hateful comments from trolls. Author and comedian Lindy West has written about the cyber mobs that have targeted her. She often writes about feminism and misogyny, or hatred of women. In response, West has received hundreds of rape threats. One troll started a fake Twitter account pretending to be her father, who had passed away recently. He even used a photo of her father on the account.

West had been told many times to just ignore trolls. However, she was so angry about the fake Twitter account that she wrote an article for *Jezebel* about how upset it made her. The next morning, she received an e-mail from the troll. He said he had not realized until then that she was a person with feelings. He admitted, "I think my anger towards you stems from your happiness with your own being. It offended me because it served to highlight my unhappiness with my own self."[19] The troll deleted the Twitter account that used West's father's name and donated money to the hospital that had treated her father. Although this incident ended well, West eventually left Twitter because of the constant harassment from other trolls and cyber mobs.

Another writer left Twitter after trolls threatened her daughter. Jessica Valenti also writes about feminism and received harassment online, including graphic rape and death threats, after everything she wrote. Like many women on the Internet, she would report the abuse but not let it stop her. One day in 2016, Valenti received a rape and death threat directed at her five-year-old daughter. After that, Valenti took a break from Twitter for several months and the threat was investigated by the Federal Bureau of Investigation (FBI). However, the abuse of other women online continues.

Zoe Quinn, shown here, was the first woman to be targeted during #Gamergate.

In 2014, women working in the gaming industry were targeted by a cyber mob. The harassment started when a game designer, Zoe Quinn, created a text-based game called *Depression Quest*. Many gamers claimed they were harassing Quinn because they disliked the game, but most outside observers said the true reason was likely because Quinn was a woman. Chat logs released from 4chan showed that some members of the cyber mob were making comments about how they did not care about *Depression Quest*, they just wanted to destroy Quinn's life and get her to commit suicide.

The harassment escalated after Quinn's ex-boyfriend wrote online that she had cheated on him with five other men. Since one of the men briefly mentioned *Depression Quest* in an article he had written, the cyber mob decided Quinn had done this to get a good review for *Depression Quest*, so they began sending her death threats and started using the hashtag #Gamergate on social media. The man spoke out to say that he had written the article before dating Quinn and noted that he did not review the game, he simply mentioned that it existed. None of this mattered to the mob; Quinn was doxed and had to leave her home to protect her safety. Eventually, #Gamergate spread from targeting Quinn to targeting any women who spoke up about sexism in the gaming industry. #Gamergate ended up proving many of the things women in the industry had complained about.

Anita Sarkeesian, the founder of Feminist Frequency—an organization that posted videos about women in gaming—was another target of the #Gamergate cyber mob. Nude photographs of Quinn and Sarkeesian began to appear online. The cyber mob made false statements about the women, including implying they were sexually promiscuous. Other women were targeted simply for criticizing #Gamergate. Brianna Wu, the owner of a gaming company, began receiving online threats after she tweeted about #Gamergate in a joking manner. She, too, left her home and work and went into hiding. Gamer and actress Felicia Day was doxed just minutes after posting online that she was afraid to talk about #Gamergate for fear of retaliation. Members of the cyber mob denied that they were targeting women simply for being women, but former professional football player Chris Kluwe pointed out that he and other men were not doxed for criticizing the cyber mob.

Later on, Quinn and Sarkeesian responded to #Gamergate by fighting back against the cyber mob. Quinn co-founded an online group called Crash Override, which helps other victims of cyber harassment. Sarkeesian used her website and videos on Feminist Frequency to expose the cyber mob and help other women fight bullies online.

LGBT+ Targets of Cyber Mobs

Members of the LGBT+ (which includes people who identify as lesbian, gay, bisexual, transgender, or another sexual orientation) community are often a target of cyber mobs. The community includes people who are questioning their sexuality and those who do not consider themselves to belong to one gender or the other. In cultures that believe LGBT+ people are bad, they are often targeted for hate speech and hate crimes. Although there has been more acceptance of LGBT+ people in the past few years, they are still likely to be harassed online for their sexuality. In some cases, the harassment is so hurtful that they commit suicide.

Harassment in the Sports World

For women who work in sports media, harassment is common. Unlike male sports reporters who receive mean comments based on their reporting of a game, female reporters receive tweets or comments on their articles that focus on their weight, sexuality, femininity, and beauty. They often receive threats of rape or abuse.

Female athletes are also a constant target of harassment. Professional golfer Paige Spiranac began to get comments on social media from trolls after she participated in a tournament in 2015. They did not focus on how she had played in the tournament; they attacked her looks, claimed that she was promiscuous, and said cruel things about her family and friends. When Spiranac talked about the harassment a year later, she cried at the memory of how hurtful it was.

Female sports stars are not the only ones who are cyberbullied. Olympic diver Tom Daley received hateful tweets after the 2016 Olympics. Daley, who dives for the British team, said before the Olympics that he was competing in memory of his father who had died earlier that year. After Daley did not win a medal, one 17-year-old Twitter user tweeted that Daley had let his dad down. The 17-year-old later tried to apologize, saying he was upset about the loss of a medal but did not want people to hate him for what he had said. British police arrested him and issued a harassment warning.

Tyler Clementi was a freshman at Rutgers University in New York City when he became the target of a cyber mob. His roommate at Rutgers University used a webcam to film Clementi on a date with another young man. The roommate then posted the video to Twitter and encouraged others to harass Clementi for being gay. A cyber mob began targeting Clementi with anti-gay hate speech and told him he should commit suicide. Unfortunately, Clementi did commit suicide not long after. The roommate was later charged with a crime for videotaping Clementi and distributing the material. He was convicted by a jury, but the conviction was overturned by a higher appeals court. He served 20 days in jail and was ordered to pay $10,000 to an anti-hate crimes organization to support work against cyber harassment.

PROTECTING LGBT+ YOUTH

"LGBT youth continue to face extraordinary obstacles in their day-to-day lives whether at school or online, but the Internet can be a valuable source of information and support when they have no one or nowhere else left to turn to. As social media evolve, so must our efforts to serve LGBT youth to ensure their safety, health and well-being."
–Dr. Eliza Byard, executive director of GLSEN

Quoted in "GLSEN's 'Out Online: The Experiences of Lesbian, Gay, Bisexual and Transgender Youth,' First National Report to Look in Depth at LGBT Youth Experience Online," GLSEN, July 10, 2013, www.glsen.org/press/study-finds-lgbt-youth-face-greater-harassment-online.

Transgender people are also likely to be targets of cyber harassment. Some transgender people do not want others to know they are transgender. When cyberbullies reveal this fact online, it can lead to physical violence against transgender people who may have been keeping their identity hidden for safety reasons.

When someone doxes a transgender person, the harassment can become deadly. The National Coalition of Anti-Violence Programs reported that "in 2013, 72 percent of all LGBT Americans murdered in hate crimes were transgender women, and 67 percent were transgender women of color."[20] Transgender people often change their names when they transition, and stolen information may contain their previous name. When doxers release this information, a cyber mob may use the former name to cause pain to the transgender person. This is called deadnaming. This disrespectful use of a person's previous name can be especially cruel because of the

Vigils are often held for members of the LGBT+ community who commit suicide because they were bullied.

discrimination many transgender people face in society, even from their own friends and family. If it becomes known at their work that they are transgender, they may lose their job.

Additionally, transgender people may have horrible memories associated with their old name. Hearing it again can cause emotional pain. Other transgender people may have changed their name to get away from an abusive partner or parents. By doxing their previous name, the cyber mob can put transgender people in the path of harm.

Deadnaming can also be used to create fake accounts to harass someone. The cyber mob may use the former name of a transgender person to create new social media accounts. When someone creates an account to impersonate someone else online, it is called a sock puppet account.

People with Disabilities

People with physical disabilities, mental health issues, learning difficulties, and emotional or behavioral difficulties have also been targeted by cyber mobs. Most harassment of people with disabilities happens both online and offline by people they know. In fact, most bullying starts face to face and then moves online.

Lizzie Velasquez had grown up with kids making fun of her. She has a rare disease that affects her eyes, heart, and bones. She is unable to gain weight, so she weighs only 63 pounds (28.5 kg). By high school, she thought she was past the bullying. However, when she was 17, Velasquez found a video on YouTube called "World's Ugliest Woman" that was about her. In the comments, most people said she did not deserve to live because of how she looked. They dehumanized her by calling her "it" instead of "she."

Velasquez said the cyberbullying felt like people were physically punching her with their words, but she was strong enough to turn the pain of being cyberbullied into work to help others. Today, she gives talks on how to help people who are victims of bullies. Velasquez spreads awareness that people with disabilities are just like everyone else. They have feelings and can be hurt by cruel words. She may be the most well-known activist against cyberbullying with memes or photos. Sometimes her picture is still circulated on the Internet with cruel captions on it. Anyone who shares these pictures is participating in a cyber mob and contributing to the pain Velasquez faces.

Motivational speaker Lizzie Velasquez (shown here) is still sometimes the victim of cyber mobs.

In 2015, Velasquez joined Tumblr's Post It Forward campaign, which allows people to support each other in their struggle against issues such as bullying, self-harm, and mental disorders. Anyone can post a video, photo, work of art, blog entry, or other form of expression and tag it with #PostItForward to share their story or messages of support and love for others.

Religious Discrimination

After the terrorist attacks of September 11, 2001, many Muslims were targeted for harassment. Many Muslim women wear a hijab, or scarf that covers their hair, so they were easy targets for people on the street. With the rise of the Internet, much of the harassment moved online. Threats to Muslims often center on false ideas about their religious beliefs. Muslim women who post pictures of themselves wearing a hijab are often flooded with messages from anonymous accounts that focus not only on their religion but also on their gender. One Muslim woman on Twitter received more than 100 death and rape threats within an hour of a cyber mob forming to harass her.

Jewish people have also long been targets of abuse, and in the digital age, Jews have become a target of cyber mobs. During the 2016 U.S. presidential election, anti-Semites created a cyber mob to attack Jewish journalists. The anti-Semitic cyber mob would identify a Jewish reporter and then begin to harass them on Twitter. When a Jewish reporter for *Newsweek*, Kurt Eichenwald, wrote about the harassment he received, the threats began to target his family and children. Eichenwald, who also suffers from epilepsy—a disorder that causes seizures—received a video from the cyber mob that had strobing lights, which are known to cause seizures in epileptics. Luckily, Eichenwald was able to drop his computer before the video caused a seizure.

Even after the election was over, Eichenwald continued to receive disturbing images and threats. In December 2016, Eichenwald received another video intended to give him an epileptic seizure. This time, it worked. Eichenwald and his wife filed a police report, and the suspect was arrested on multiple federal charges, including cyberstalking.

Teens and Privacy

The Internet has become a large part of socializing, but this also makes teenagers and young children vulnerable to cyber harassment. It can take place on social media, through text messaging, and even through video games. While adults are most often targeted by anonymous strangers, children and teenagers are more often bullied online by friends or people from school.

One way teenagers may be targeted is by someone sharing their personal photos. Sometimes, young couples send nude photos to each other. However, even when both people are willingly participating, they can be charged with possessing child pornography if they are under 18. Additionally, they must remember that the person they are sending the photo to will always have it unless they choose to delete it. Even on apps such as Snapchat, where the photo disappears after a short amount of time, someone can take a screenshot. The app lets people know when someone takes a screenshot, but this does not help the person get the picture back.

When a couple breaks up, some people may share nude photos of their ex to get back at them for breaking off the relationship. Some websites post photos of unwilling victims—mostly young women—to shame them. Sometimes, they charge the women a fee to take the photos down, which is known as extortion—an illegal practice where someone gains money through threats or violence. However, by the time victims find out they are on these websites, the images are often spread across the Internet and almost impossible to remove completely.

Private Photos

According to the Cyber Civil Rights Initiative (CCRI),

The term "revenge porn," though frequently used, is somewhat misleading. Many perpetrators are not motivated by revenge or by any personal feelings toward the victim. A more accurate term is nonconsensual pornography (NCP), defined as the distribution of sexually graphic images of individuals without their consent.[1]

The CCRI has a helpful website that explains how to delete nonconsensual images on all the major social media websites. Steps include documenting the post, unfriending or disconnecting from the person who posted the photo, and reporting it to the social media company and law enforcement.

In the United States, 38 states and the District of Columbia have laws against NCP. The laws are different across the states. For instance, in New Hampshire, the nonconsensual sharing of photos is a felony; in Alabama, the first offense is a misdemeanor, and any more offenses are felonies; in Arkansas, all offenses are misdemeanors. The punishment for a felony is generally a jail sentence of one year or more. A misdemeanor is generally punishable by a fine or jail sentence of less than a year.

1. Cyber Civil Rights Initiative, 2017. www.cybercivilrights.org

Cyber Mobs and Celebrities

Famous people are often targeted by cyber mobs. Many celebrities have social media accounts where they can interact with fans and talk about issues that are important to them. This openness and connectivity can make them easy targets for hatred. In 2016, African American actress and comedian Leslie Jones was forced off Twitter for a period of time by an angry mob. Their cruel tweets to her were mainly racist and sexist in nature.

Actress Leslie Jones was targeted by a cyber mob on Twitter because she is a black woman. Attacks against black women are sometimes called "misogynoir," a combination of "misogyny" (hatred of women) and "noir" (the French word for "black").

Jones tried many times to report the abuse to Twitter. Some people told her to just ignore the hateful tweets, but she said the trolls deserved to be reported to Twitter. The company has a policy about abusive language and eventually banned the leader of the mob, Milo Yiannopoulos, from its platform. However, Twitter was criticized for not stopping the abuse more quickly.

Many other celebrities have had similar issues with cyber mobs. Some have chosen to shut down their social media or put their Internet use on hold until cyber mobs choose a different target. When they return to the Internet, the abusive posts may still be there. Material posted by cyber mobs on social media websites is often flagged by users but not removed. In high-profile cyber mob attacks such as Jones's experience, social media websites can be motivated to remove content, but if people are not famous, their experience may never be brought to the website's attention.

Other times, celebrities can encourage cyber mobs, either directly or indirectly. In October 2015, when Donald Trump was campaigning for president, a young woman named Lauren Batchelder asked him questions at a political forum about abortion access and equal pay for women. Trump answered her questions but later tweeted that she was an "arrogant young woman" who questioned him in "such a nasty fashion."[21] He also falsely accused her of being a member of the staff of his opponent, Jeb Bush.

Although Trump did not tell people to harass Batchelder, his tweets encouraged many of his supporters to do so. They posted her phone number and other personal information online, and she received hundreds of threatening phone calls, e-mails, and Facebook messages. This shows the power a celebrity's actions can have; when Trump attacked Batchelder, he unknowingly started a cyber mob.

CYBER MOBS COMMIT CRIMES

"It is not a scandal. It is a sex crime. It is a sexual violation ... Anybody who looked at those pictures, you're perpetrating a sexual offense."
—Jennifer Lawrence, actress

Quoted in Sam Kashner, "Both Huntress and Prey," Vanity Fair, November 2014. www.vanityfair.com/hollywood/2014/10/jennifer-lawrence-photo-hacking-privacy.

Celebrities, especially female ones, are often the targets of hacking campaigns that steal personal photographs in an effort to embarrass them or damage their reputation. In 2014, members of 4chan broke into the online documents of a number of female celebrities. The hackers were able to steal the women's nude photos and then spread them to other websites, including Twitter. Actress Jennifer Lawrence was one of the women affected. Lawrence told *Vanity Fair* magazine, "I was just so afraid. I didn't know how this would affect my career."[22] Lawrence and other celebrities affected by the theft worked with the FBI to try to recover the stolen photos and punish the thieves.

CHAPTER 5

Combating Cyber Attacks

Cyber mobs can be difficult to fight, so the best defense is a good offense: Everyone should be sure to protect their information with strong passwords and privacy settings, and it is wise to think twice before posting something that might be seen as controversial. Many people do not like the fact that the burden of preventing attacks tends to fall on the potential victims, but until laws regulating crime on the Internet are improved and enforced, it will continue to be difficult to bring cyber mobs to justice.

There are many organizations that focus on helping victims of cyber mobs feel better able to deal with online abuse. Activists against online hate have developed ways for victims to regain some opportunities to engage online. These tactics include forming counter-mobs and counter-hacking to support a victim or expose members of the cyber mob. New groups have developed to teach victims about current laws that may help them combat cyber abuse. Free online guides to protecting information and passwords have been created, and new technology is being created every day to help stop cyber mobs.

Protecting Information Online

Protecting information online can be difficult, but it is important for keeping power out of the hands of cyber mobs. Experts recommend creating a different difficult password for every account and using more than one e-mail address. Some websites offer two-factor authentication. This means that when someone signs into the account, the website will send a special code to the cell phone on record. Having to take two steps to sign in prevents someone without access to both the password and the cell phone from logging in.

Social media accounts can be restricted so that only friends can view the content. This will limit the ways a cyber mob can reach someone. It is always a good idea to keep some personal information off a profile, such as address, workplace, or school.

If someone does become the victim of a cyber attack, they should document their abusers' posts. When harassing accounts are blocked online by a victim, the past harassment can often no longer be seen by the victim. This can be both good and bad. People being harassed do not want to see the cruel messages again, but having proof of a cyber mob attack is important. If a victim goes to the police to report the harassment, it is important to have a copy of the messages.

Online Protection Resources

Protecting private information online can seem like an impossible task, but some groups have resources that can help. The Department of Homeland Security (DHS) has put together resources on its website. The cyber security campaign, called Stop.Think.Connect., provides information for students, parents, and more. Stop.Think.Connect. offers tips on how to avoid accidentally downloading spy software, or malware, to a computer. It also offers tips on secure connections to Wi-Fi, home networks, and school networks.

Another organization that gives specific tips for online protection is HACK*BLOSSOM. This company wrote "A DIY Guide to Feminist Cybersecurity" to help women and men protect themselves online. This guide covers areas such as cell phones, web browsers, and changing the settings in social media apps.

A third group, called Webbing with Wisdom, teaches women and girls what cyberstalking looks like and how to report it. The group also discusses all the ways cyberbullying can happen on social media and gives tips for protecting private documents.

Counter-Speech

Groups that are normally the targets of cyber mobs and cyberbullying have been effective in promoting counter-speech. Counter-speech means using words that challenge the messages of hatred by presenting counterarguments, facts, or even calling out the hatred for what it is. Counter-speech can be when people use the words of the cyber mob against it through either parody or elevation to the attention of others. By bringing the cyber mob to the attention of the wider public, counter-speech can show victims that they are not alone and that the cyber mob's views are not socially accepted.

During the second debate of the 2016 presidential election, Donald Trump called on Muslims to report suspicious behavior by other Muslims. Trump had previously called for the deportation of Muslims from the United States, which many thought was threatening language. Instead of giving in to the fear created by the call to watch their neighbors, Muslims on Twitter quickly reacted with counter-speech. They created a hashtag called #MuslimsReportStuff and used it to report things such as their father taking a nap after dinner, their dislike of kale as a vegetable, and specifically, reports about Trump acting threatening on the debate stage. By mocking his call for surveillance on Muslims with this self-reporting, Muslims helped counter the attitude that they may be dangerous as a group. Through the hashtag, Muslims were able to use humor to defend against discrimination.

Muslims used the hashtag #MuslimsReportStuff to show that they are just like other Americans.

FREE SPEECH IS IMPORTANT

"Having the opportunity to engage as a citizen and to participate in the creation of culture is one of the central reasons why we protect speech."
–Danielle Keats Citron, author and cyber harassment expert

Danielle Keats Citron. *Hate Crimes in Cyberspace*. Cambridge, MA: Harvard University Press, 2014, p. 193.

Emily Lindin was a victim of bullies while she was growing up. They spread rumors about her in school and harassed her. As an adult, Lindin read about a number of young women who committed suicide after being harassed by online mobs. In response, she started the UnSlut Project in 2013 to help promote gender equality and sex education. The UnSlut Project allows anyone to share their story and learn from each other. "These shared stories not only provide hope and solidarity to girls who are currently suffering," Lindin wrote, "they demonstrate to us all just how widespread the issues of sexual bullying and 'slut' shaming really are."[23]

A group of activists got together in 2015 to define the fight against cyber mobs and cyber bullies. They gathered at the International Workshop on Misogyny and the Internet. The workshop defined counter-speech as "exposing hate, deceit, abuse, stereotypes," in addition to "providing clarification and promoting counter narratives" and "advancing counter-values: sharing experiences and uniting communities."[24]

Another form of counter-speech is taking place in the world of sports media. Women in this field often receive cruel and harassing tweets and other online messages. To draw attention to this problem, three men in sports media are fighting back. Brad Burke, Gareth Hughes, Joe Reed, and Adam Woullard run a podcast called *Just Not Sports*, where they speak to athletes and sports media personalities about the things they like besides sports. To fight cyber harassment of women in sports, *Just Not Sports* produced a video called "#MoreThanMean" where everyday men read mean tweets that female sports reporters had received. They read the tweets sitting face to face with the woman who originally received the abuse. In the video, the tweets started out with mild insults, but quickly turned into rape and death threats. The men could not look at the women anymore and asked if they were required to read the tweets out loud. By reading the harassment while looking at the victim, the men were able to understand the effect cyber harassment has on a real person. The words that normally lose meaning on a computer screen had come to life, and the men—as well as everyone watching the video—could see the real consequences.

When people can see the effect their words have on another person, they are less likely to be cruel.

Counter-speech does not return hate with hate or try to personally attack members of a cyber mob. Instead, it works to change the conversation by providing support for victims, showing respect for everyone involved, and challenging ideas that are hurtful. Counter-speech may not be able to directly prove statements incorrect, but it can work to show everyone involved that civility and mutual respect are important parts of any discussion.

Some people have grouped together to create counter-mobs. These groups work to help victims of cyber mobs by identifying the bullies. They also work using counter-speech with the same volume as a cyber mob. Instead of one person standing up to a cyber mob, there may be hundreds of posts telling a cyber mob to stop the harassment. Counter-mobs drown out the cyber mob with messages of support for the victim. This kind of counter-attack can help victims feel less alone and force cyber mob participants to realize their ideas are not as supported as they thought.

By using counter-hacking and other research, trolls' real names can be identified. Some victims have started finding a troll's real name and then researching to find someone in their life who might hold them accountable. Victims will send these people a screenshot of the online content written by a troll. Trolls may then face many of the same consequences as the victim of a cyber mob. They could lose jobs, be suspended in school, or be in trouble with parents or partners. However, some people feel this kind of behavior is no better than what the trolls do.

Does Shaming Bullies Help?

Researcher Dr. Brené Brown believes shaming someone might actually make their behavior worse:

Based on my research and the research of other shame researchers, I believe that there is a profound difference between shame and guilt. I believe that guilt is adaptive and helpful—it's holding something we've done or failed to do up against our values and feeling psychological discomfort.

I define shame as the intensely painful feeling or experience of believing that we are flawed and therefore unworthy of love and belonging—something we've experienced, done, or failed to do makes us unworthy of connection.

I don't believe shame is helpful or productive. In fact, I think shame is much more likely to be the source of destructive, hurtful behavior than the solution or cure. I think the fear of disconnection can make us dangerous.[1]

To fight online bullies, counter-speech and other measures should focus on creating a feeling of guilt in the abusers, rather than shaming them. Helping cyberbullies understand why their behavior is wrong may help them overcome the need to be cruel. Instead of feeling ashamed as a person, they can take responsibility for their behaviors and make changes.

1. Brené Brown, "Shame v. Guilt," Brené Brown, January 14, 2013, brenebrown.com/2013/01/14/2013114-shame-v-guilt-html/

Laws Regarding Privacy

In May 2014, the European Court of Justice, representing member countries of the European Union (EU), ruled on a case about privacy on the Internet. The case had been brought by a Spanish citizen who found online information about a past event to be negatively influencing his current life. The citizen sued Google for the right to remove now false information from being found when someone searched for him. The EU Court ruled in his favor. "Individuals have the right—under certain conditions—to ask search engines to remove links with personal information about them. This applies where the information is inaccurate, inadequate, irrelevant or excessive for the purposes of the data processing."[25] After the ruling, the EU sought to strengthen it and made sure that the "Right to Be Forgotten" existed for all EU citizens. According to Ronson, 70,000 people applied to be forgotten within the first three months of the ruling.

There are limits to the deletion of search results. Criminals may not use the ruling to erase information about their conviction even after serving their time in jail. An example of something that can be "forgotten" is a newspaper article that falsely identified someone as a criminal. In this case, Google and other search engines must remove the article from searches for the innocent person.

The United States does not have a law such as this one. There are services that can push positive search results to the top of a search engine's results, but they are generally more expensive than the average person can afford. Any embarrassing or false information posted by others can be seen by anyone, including friends, school administrators, and future employers.

In 2015, California enacted a law for minors who want to remove content from the Internet. The California Rights for Minors in the Digital World Act (Senate Bill 568), or Online Eraser law, allows people under the age of 18 who live in California to remove content from websites and social media apps, even those based outside of California. Every website that allows young people to upload material must have a way for them to delete the information. This content can be photos or text posts that no longer represent them or could come to harm their future work and school prospects. The law only covers websites that are used by minors, not any content on websites directed at people over the age of 18, such as dating apps. Some people support this law, while others feel it is too confusing to be helpful. *The Week* explained,

> *For example, the law does not require companies to remove content copied or posted by a third party. So if an Instagram user posts an embarrassing image of a fellow Instagram user who is 15 years old, Instagram would not have to honor the 15-year-old's request to remove the embarrassing image because she did not post the image herself. And even if the embarrassing image was originally posted by the 15-year-old and then reposted by another Instagram user, Instagram would still not have to remove the image.*[26]

One law firm in New York City, which is run by lawyer Carrie Goldberg, focuses on cases that involve Internet abuse and sexual consent. Goldberg and her firm help gather evidence, track down cyber mob participants, and bring the cases to court. They also work to remove photos from the Internet by monitoring nonconsensual pornography websites and reporting content. This can be endless work for one person and emotionally difficult for a victim to do on their own. The firm provides this service to help victims recover their online lives and their emotional stability. Goldberg told Whitman College, "We have clients who have never even taken a naked picture before but were, for instance, filmed without their consent or knowledge, ... Photoshopped onto a porn star's body, or even, sadly, recorded while being sexually assaulted."[27]

Filming someone without their consent in a place where they have a reason to expect privacy—for instance, in a changing room or in their own home—is illegal.

Governments in other countries are also taking steps to stop online harassment. In Germany, the government asked social media companies to remove any hate speech within 24 hours. This should help social media companies develop better algorithms, which could help identify abuse for humans to review. Eventually, it might even be able to delete the worst posts so no human has to read them. For now, people still have to flag any hate speech they see, and then staff members at Facebook will review it and decide whether to delete it.

A Code of Conduct

Some people believe the entire Internet needs a code of conduct. The Internet Society, a nonprofit organization that aims to keep the Internet safe and open for everyone, has written one for its members. It includes making sure work done on the Internet does not hurt anyone. The code also talks about how to keep the Internet open to everyone by not making technology that keeps people away. The most important part of the code asks that everyone follow the norms of Internet etiquette, or what most people consider an acceptable way to behave. For instance, it is considered a violation of etiquette to post unkind things about someone online. A universal code of ethics could remind everyone that even online, other people have rights and deserve respect.

A code of conduct or ethics could help protect Internet speech. It could also help make the Internet a better place. By reminding everyone of their rights and responsibilities, these codes might change the way people act online.

Outside Help and Protecting Others

There are many organizations that support victims of cyber mobs. These groups put together websites, books, and sometimes apps to help people deal with cyber abuse. There are also apps that help report and stop cyberbullying. One of these apps is called STOPit. STOPit lets any user take a picture of cyber harassment and anonymously send the picture to someone who can help. Most STOPit users are children or teens. They can report cyberbullying directly to their parents or school so an adult can step in and help.

In schools, most teachers are trained to look for bullying among their students, but they are not always aware of what is happening online. Additionally, schools cannot monitor the private e-mails or social media of their students. However, they can see anything that is made public. Some schools have started looking at public social media profiles for evidence of bullying, but this has led to controversy as people argue that the school should not be able to punish students for posts that are made outside of school. In one case, four California students were suspended after "liking" a racist post on Instagram in March 2017. The post appeared to threaten violence against two black members of the school; one was a student, and the other was a coach. After the students were suspended, they sued the school for violating their right to free speech. Many people are unsure of how much power schools should have over students, especially when it comes to things that are posted on the Internet, and it is a subject that is likely to be debated for some time.

Most parents want to help their children deal with bullying, but many do not know all the ways kids can be bullied. They may not even know the names of some social media websites or apps. This can make it hard to understand the problem when their children report bullying. One U.S. government agency is trying to change that. The Substance Abuse and Mental Health Services Administration (SAMHSA) created an app just for parents called KnowBullying. Parents can download the app and learn about bullying and the Internet. This kind of education can help parents support kids who are being bullied online or in school.

CHAPTER 6

The Future of Cyber Harassment

Cyber mobs have increased in recent years, but so have the ways they can be stopped. People working against cyber mobs are developing new technology every day to help keep the Internet a safe place to share ideas. Lawyers and police officers are working together with community groups to learn current laws and create new laws to prosecute cyber mobs. In the fight against cyber mobs, everyone online has a part to play. Every day, people online are becoming more aware of digital citizenship and the power of helping each other fight hate.

Improving Technology

For several years now, many websites have given users the ability to report abuse when they see it. Additionally, some websites use volunteers to make sure the policies of the website, especially regarding cruel or offensive speech, are not broken. These volunteers are referred to as moderators, or mods. Some may be more strict in their interpretation of the policies than others. The company employees generally only get involved when the company could be at risk for a lawsuit over something posted by users. Other websites use artificial intelligence, or AI, instead of real people. AI uses algorithms to act like humans would online. These AI programs can be bots (short for robots), scripts, or other software that steps in to identify and delete abusive posts.

Henry Lieberman, a computer scientist at the Massachusetts Institute of Technology (MIT), is hoping to stop cyberbullying and provide resources for victims. He and his research team are developing new tools to make online spaces safer. Based on computer programs that are already in use, Lieberman hopes to change online behavior. One program he and his team are looking to mimic is already being researched for Facebook. Currently, Facebook users can report when a friend's status seems to indicate that they are suicidal. If the user clicks on the arrow to the upper right of the post, reports the post, and clicks on "I don't think this should be on Facebook" as the reason why, a list of options will appear that the user can choose from, including that the post appears suicidal. If the Facebook team agrees after they see the post, they will send the friend a popup box offering support through a friend or helpline. Eventually, Facebook hopes to develop the technology to the point where it can identify suicidal posts without needing anyone to report them.

Lieberman and his team are working to develop similar algorithms for bullying. They researched bullying posts online and found that many were focused on the same six topics: physical looks, intelligence, race, ethnicity, sexuality, and social acceptance or rejection. The new algorithm would look for these topics and then show a popup before the user can post it. For instance, if a user is about to post something mean, the popup might ask the person to reconsider posting or make them wait 60 seconds to post so they have time to think about their statement. Lieberman hopes reminding users of the power of their language could stop some bullies.

Lieberman also hopes this program can help victims of bullying. It can be difficult for kids who are being bullied to reach out to an adult or talk to their friends. The popup for bullying victims might ask if they need help and provide a clickable resource. Lieberman is also working with MTV on a campaign called A Thin Line. The campaign's website helps people identify behavior they may not have recognized as bullying as well as find and talk with others who have had similar experiences.

In an 18-month study published in 2016, researchers from Stanford and Cornell Universities looked at 40 million comments on 3 websites: news website CNN, political website Breitbart, and gaming website IGN. The study concluded that it might be possible to predict troll-like behavior before it happens. Trolls used worse grammar, posted more often, and received more replies than the average user, indicating that what they were saying was sparking controversy. The researchers created an algorithm that

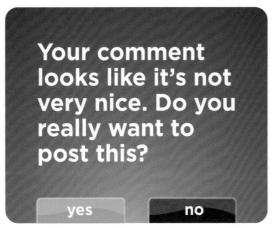

Henry Lieberman and his research team are hoping to create an algorithm that would identify harassing speech and show trolls a popup box similar to this one.

can search for these patterns in posts and identify within 10 posts whether someone should be banned from a website. Without the algorithm, the researchers found, trolls were generally able to post more than 250 times before they were banned. A website moderator would still need to review the posts to make sure the algorithm is correct, but it should be able to alert them to the presence of trolls more quickly.

In 2016, the Google-owned company Jigsaw developed a set of tools called Conversation AI, which looks for abusive language at the moment it is posted. It is designed to learn from abusive comments and give future comments a score out of 100, with 100 being the most offensive. Jigsaw said that Conversation AI would be tested on the *New York Times* website comments, blocking abuse until a moderator can review the comment. If it works well, other websites may start using it.

Some people approve of software such as Conversation AI and believe it should be used across the Internet to shut down cyber mobs before they start. However, others fear it will lead to too much censorship. *Wired* magazine pointed out some of the problems with Conversation AI:

> During her worst days of being targeted by a gang of misogynists last year, feminist writer Sady Doyle would look down at her phone after an hour and find a hundred new Twitter notifications, many of them crude sexual comments and attacks on her history of mental health issues. But when I present her with the notion of Conversation AI as a solution, she hesitates. "People need to be able to talk in whatever register they talk," she says. "Imagine what the Internet would be like if you couldn't say '[The president] is a moron.'" In fact, when I run the phrase through the Conversation AI prototype, I find that calling someone a moron scores a full 99 out of 100 on its personal attack scale.

The example highlights Conversation AI's potential for false positives or suppressing the gray areas of speech. After all, even without automated flagging, Twitter and Facebook have been criticized for blocking legitimate, even politically powerful, content: ... [For example,] Facebook blocked photos of drowned migrant children intended to make Americans more aware of the tragedy of Syria's refugee crisis.[28]

Many people support the creation of a program such as Conversation AI but believe it should not be able to automatically delete things, otherwise the potential for censorship is too great. They feel a real person still needs to review the things these programs flag and unflag them if they are not cruel or harmful. Balancing moderation and free speech is a tricky thing, and even humans still have trouble with it; robots are not advanced enough yet to do it on their own.

On Twitter, humans are using technology to distract trolls. Twitter user Sarah Nyberg created a bot to automatically respond to harassment. Its script, like an algorithm, responds in pre-determined ways when it sees certain language. It is programmed to make statements that trolls tend to argue with, such as, "Affirmative action doesn't oppress white people."[29] According to Nyberg, one troll argued with the bot for 10 hours straight, thinking it was a human. Distracting the troll this way meant he or she could not target a real person, and many people found it funny to see someone arguing with a bot. Nyberg's original goal was "to expose the hypocrisy of the sorts of people who say 'feminists' and 'social justice warriors' are hypersensitive. Even just mild statements of fact can have them absolutely freak out—and end up sending abuse, even—to a bot that responds calmly and just explains over and over again that they're wrong."[30] Nyberg's experiment also proved that trolls generally seek fights; to find the bot, they had to search for the kinds of comments it was making.

Twitter users can also create a list of accounts to block. They can send this list to other people so individuals being targeted by harassers can join together to block the harassment. This kind of technology could be developed for other social media.

Strengthening Current Laws

There are many current laws that could be used to stop cyber mobs and their harassment tactics, but these can only be enforced if the harassers can be identified. Since many people hide their identity online, this can be difficult. Additionally, the American legal system is often difficult for people to figure out, and legal fees tend to be expensive. To some people, it is not worth the time, effort, and money it takes to bring a court case against someone. However, for others, the harassment is so harmful that they need to take action. Lawmakers are currently looking at ways to change existing laws so they can better protect people from online harassment.

One way to stop online harassment with photos and videos is to use current copyright laws. Copyright means that someone—generally the person who took the picture—is the owner of an image. If the victim of cyber harassment took a nude photograph and that photograph is spread around the Internet or used in a harassing way, the victim may be able to use copyright laws to have the image removed. However, this can be a long, difficult, and expensive process, and sometimes, images remain on the Internet or personal computers.

According to the Pew Research Center, "The U.S. Telecommunications Act of 1996 does not hold websites responsible for content posted by users, leaving technology companies to create and enforce their own community standards."[31] Many believe this law should be changed to make technology companies responsible for what people do on their websites. Others believe this would silence legitimate free speech by forcing technology companies to censor important ideas.

THE INTERNET CAN BE HELPFUL OR HARMFUL

"It's ironic: The same technology that connects the world and thereby can help teach people to understand and respect one another can also be used by those who want to foment intolerance and violence, spreading hatred across international borders."
–Abraham H. Foxman and Christopher Wolf, authors

Abraham H. Foxman and Christopher Wolf, *Viral Hate: Containing Its Spread on the Internet.* New York, NY: Palgrave Macmillan, 2013, p. 28.

When cyber mobs pretend they are the victim, it is called impersonation. It is a crime to knowingly impersonate another person for the purpose of harming them. In 2012, a young man in Toronto, Canada, created a Facebook account impersonating another student at his school. The young man then posted statements claiming to hate his parents and friends, as well as other cruel remarks. The poster was using this fake account to turn the victim's friends and family against him as a way of cyberbullying. The fake account was active for 11 months until the police got involved.

Providing Training

There is a great need for more lawyers and police officers to be trained in how to respond to online hate and cyber mobs. Some advocacy groups in the United States have developed courses for police and legal advocates. For instance, the Tyler Clementi Institute for CyberSafety trains lawyers on how to represent victims of cyberbullying and uses research to educate judges, lawmakers, and the public about cyber mobs.

Other groups work with police officers and community groups to learn the signs of cyberbullying and the best ways to help a victim. Victims of cyber mobs can feel alone when a mob is attacking. If they decide to reach out to a school counselor, teacher, or police officer, these helpers need to know how to respond.

Better training is needed for law enforcement officials so they know how to proceed when an online crime is reported.

A 1998 federal law called the Children's Online Privacy Protection Act (COPPA) tries to help parents control the information available on the Internet about their children under age 13. This law helps parents remove information and photos of their children online. Another U.S. law that may help victims of cyber harassment is the interstate stalking statute, or Section 2261A. The law states that any behavior that "causes, attempts to cause, or would be reasonably expected to cause substantial emotional distress to a person"[32] is punishable. The law covers harassment by any computer service or other electronic communication.

Making New Laws

While there are laws punishing human rights violations already on record, many of these laws do not cover online life. According to Mary Traina, who wrote an article for *The Cut* about her experience being cyberstalked for more than 10 years, "The biggest obstacle to effective legislation is that officials simply don't understand how to proceed when a crime is reported."[33] To address this problem, Representative Katherine M. Clark of Massachusetts proposed a law called the Cybercrime Enforcement Training Assistance Act of 2016, which focused on giving police the tools and training to target cyber mobs. She also proposed the Interstate Swatting Hoax Act of 2015, which would make swatting a crime. Traina supported the idea of the Cybercrime Enforcement Assistance Act, but noted that when she tried to report her cyberstalker—first to her boss, then to the police—she was dismissed and told that her cyberstalker was probably not dangerous. The only advice she got was to ignore him and keep her address private. She said, "Maybe Clark's bill will help. But it will take more than a legislative victory to convince those in charge that unwanted advances are anything but harmless."[34]

Representative Jackie Speier of California is also trying to protect Internet users. In 2016, she proposed the Intimate Privacy Protection Act (IPPA), which makes sharing sexual photos or videos without consent a crime. The law would help prevent nonconsensual pornography. Some groups have criticized the law and others like it, claiming it would violate people's right to free speech. However, since the IPPA specifies that a crime has taken place only if the person in the photo or video has not consented for the material to be shared, experts agree the law is not unconstitutional because it protects people's privacy without violating free speech.

Other concerns about new cyber abuse laws relate to government oversight. Many feel that giving the government too much access to social media accounts to punish criminals or track terrorists could lead to innocent people being imprisoned. Laws that ban anonymity or are used to track down cyber mob members could be used to do the same to protestors or other people that a government does not approve of. This would be a restriction of free speech and free assembly and in many countries, could endanger the lives of protestors. In some countries outside the United States, people who protest against the government are watched on social media. This can lead to their arrest and sometimes death.

Facebook's Tips for Sharing

Facebook has created a bullying and safety tip center on its website that lists important rules to follow when using social media. For instance, even if users know everyone on their friends list, Facebook reminds them that anything can be shared by friends without permission. The best defense is to be careful about what is being posted. The website offered these tips:

Before you share, ask yourself:

- *Could somebody use this to hurt me?*

- *Would I be upset if someone shared this with others?*

- *What's the worst thing that could happen if I shared this?*[1]

Facebook has policies that do not allow people to share certain things, such as violent, hateful, or sexually explicit posts. However, trolls and cyber mobs do not always follow the rules, and once something has been spread around, it can be difficult or impossible to take it down from every website. This is why it is important for users to think before they post.

1. "Tools: Staying Safe," Facebook, 2017. www.facebook.com/safety/tools/safety.

Changing Trolls and the Internet

Laws that protect people are necessary and important, but some people do not have a problem with breaking the law. To make the Internet a better, safer place for everyone, people must work on changing cyber mobs' attitudes. This can be difficult to do, and there is no one single way that works for everyone; however, social experts have proposed several ideas. Sometimes, ignoring the hateful messages is the best way to deal with them, but other times, as several victims have found, confronting the cyber mob may help stop the abuse. This is because when people see the effect their words have on others, it might stop them from harassing people. However, this tactic does not work on people whose intention is to cause others harm.

Gaming brings millions of people from all walks of life together. The community should be used to help and support each other, not harass and intimidate.

Digital Citizenship

The Internet allows people to participate in a global conversation. Just like citizens of a country, everyone on the Internet has digital citizenship. With this citizenship comes a responsibility to keep the conversation open to everyone.

FLAWED BUT IMPORTANT

"Social media like Twitter and Facebook are certainly flawed, but they function as hosts for public conversations on a huge variety of social issues. If women, people of color, and LGB Internet users are shying away from contributing because of well-founded fears of retaliation, their voices will be missing from this important civic sphere. Social media doesn't necessarily have to operate this way."

–Alice Marwick, fellow at the Data & Society Research Institute

Alice Marwick, "A New Study Suggests Online Harassment Is Pressuring Women and Minorities to Self-Censor," *Quartz*, November 24, 2016. qz.com/844319/a-new-study-suggests-online-harassment-is-pressuring-women-and-minorities-to-self-censor/.

Digital citizenship means knowing the consequences of online speech and helping the community report cyber mobs. Learning about the ways that cyber mobs hurt people is important because knowledge helps good people recognize bad behavior and know how to act. Counter-speech and other tools for helping victims of cyberattacks can be learned with the help of online communities.

It is up to the people who use the Internet to report hate when they see it. When hate is reported and counter-speech is practiced regularly, the Internet becomes safer for everyone. Right now, people often feel they can say whatever they want online without consequences. A community of active digital citizens can change that. They can make it the norm to be kind and stand up for others. Being a digital citizen also means taking responsibility for privacy. This involves not sharing other people's photos or information without their consent. Only the owner of photos or information can provide this consent.

Digital citizens learn the rules of good behavior on the Internet. They do not use anonymity to hurt other people. If a digital citizen sees other people bullying, they do not join the cyber mob. They learn to recognize when their own words are hurtful. They think before they type. Digital citizens know that just because something can be done does not always mean it should be done. The Internet has rules of civility just like regular society. Good digital citizens know these rules and follow them.

When other people stand up for a victim, they may be able to change the course of a cyber mob. Fighting back with mean words only gives permission for the attacker to keep being mean. When a cyber mob attacks, sometimes the only way to fight is to remain calm and kind.

Be an Upstander, Not a Bystander

Empathy—the ability to understand how other people feel—is important for changing bullying. Empathetic people can help the victim of a cyber mob by becoming upstanders rather than bystanders. Bystanders watch something happen; upstanders step in to help the targets of bullying, online or off. They learn about how to recognize bullying behavior, combat rumors, and do not view pictures without consent. Upstanders reach out to the targets of bullies and cyber mobs to let them know they are not alone. Sometimes, it is not safe for an upstander to help someone directly; in that case, they can report the bullying to an adult and talk to the victim privately.

Being an upstander and a friend to victims of cyber mobs can change the Internet for the better. Hashtags such as #stopbullying or #nobullying can be spread by upstanders to help show victims they are not alone. Using this method of counter-speech, upstanders can spread love around the Internet instead of hate.

Being an upstander can feel tiring. There is a lot of hate in the world, and sometimes, people feel discouraged. They may think there is no way to help or that the job of changing the culture of the Internet is too big for them. This is called compassion fatigue, and it can happen to anyone. People need to remember that while there are a lot of bad things out there, there are also a lot of good things. Each person doing a little bit of good can help tip the scales.

Helping victims deal with cyber mobs and bullies can change and even save lives. If enough upstanders and digital citizens stand up for what is right, they can change the world.

Introduction: When Socialization Goes Wrong

1. Heinz Leymann, "Mobbing and Psychological Terror at Workplaces," *Violence and Victims* 5, vol. 5, no. 2, Springer Publishing, 1990, p. 120. www.mobbingportal.com/LeymannV&V1990(3).pdf.

2. Danielle Keats Citron, *Hate Crimes in Cyberspace*. Cambridge, MA: Harvard University Press, 2016, p. 23.

Chapter 1: The Rise of Cyber Mobs

3. "Mob—The Vicious Attack," No Bullying, May 19, 2015. nobullying. com/mob.

4. Claire Hardaker, "Trolling in Asynchronous Computer-Mediated Communication: From User Discussions to Academic Definitions," *Journal of Politeness Research*, vol. 6, no. 2, p. 224.

5. Dia Kayyali and Danny O'Brien, "Facing the Challenge of Online Harassment," Electronic Frontier Foundation, 2015. www.eff.org/ deeplinks/2015/01/facing-challenge-online-harassment.

6. *McIntyre v. Ohio Elections Commission*, 514 U.S. 334 (1995). www.law.cornell.edu/supct/html/93-986.ZO.html.

7. Students in Action, "Debating the 'Mighty Constitutional Opposites': Debating Hate Speech," American Bar Association. www.americanbar. org/groups/public_education/initiatives_awards/students_in_action/ debate_hate.html.

8. Students in Action, "Debating the 'Mighty Constitutional Opposites': Debating Hate Speech."

9. "Sedition Act Becomes Federal Law," History.com. www.history. com/this-day-in-history/sedition-act-becomes-federal-law.

10. "Privacy Policy," Tumblr, January 27, 2014. www.tumblr.com/ policy/en/privacy.

11. T.M. Scanlon, "A Theory of Freedom of Expression." *Philosophy & Public Affairs* 1 (1972): 224.

12. Frank LaRue, *Report of the Special Rapporteur on the Promotion and Protection of the Right to Freedom of Opinion and Expression*, Human Rights Council, Seventeenth Session Agenda Item 3, United Nations General Assembly, May 16, 2011. www2.ohchr.org/english/bodies/ hrcouncil/docs/17session/A.HRC.17.27_en.pdf.

Chapter 2: Harassment Types

13. Hardaker, "Trolling in Asynchronous Computer-Mediated Communication: From User Discussions to Academic Definitions."

14. Quoted in Helen Walters, "Peeking Behind the Curtain at Anonymous: Gabriella Coleman at TEDGlobal 2012," TED Blog, June 27, 2012. blog.ted.com/peeking-behind-the-curtain-at-anonymous-gabriella-coleman-at-tedglobal-2012/.

15. Quoted in Dan Tynan, "The Terror of Swatting: How the Law is Tracking Down High-Tech Prank Callers," *The Guardian*, April 15, 2016. www.theguardian.com/technology/2016/apr/15/swatting-law-teens-anonymous-prank-call-police.

Chapter 3: Consequences of Cyber Attacks

16. Kenneth Westhues, "At the Mercy of the Mob," *OHS Canada*, vol. 18, no. 8, December 2002, pp. 30-36. www.kwesthues.com/ohs-canada.htm.

17. *Rosenblatt v. Baer*, 383 U.S. 75, 86 (1966).

18. Danielle Keats Citron, "Civil Rights in Our Information Age," in *The Offensive Internet: Speech, Privacy, and Reputation*, ed. Saul Levmore and Martha Nussbaum. Cambridge, MA: Harvard University Press, 2010, p. 47.

Chapter 4: Special Issues with Protected Groups

19. Quoted in Lindy West, "What Happened When I Confronted My Cruellest Troll," *The Guardian*, February 2, 2015. www.theguardian.com/society/2015/feb/02/what-happened-confronted-cruellest-troll-lindy-west.

20. Brynn Tannehill, "Ohio and the Epidemic of Anti-Transgender Violence," *Huffington Post*, February 2, 2016. www.huffingtonpost.com/brynn-tannehill/ohio-and-the-epidemic-of-_b_6720892.html.

21. Donald J. Trump's Twitter page, October 13, 2015. twitter.com/realDonaldTrump.

22. Quoted in Sam Kashner, "Both Huntress and Prey," *Vanity Fair*, November 2014. www.vanityfair.com/hollywood/2014/10/jennifer-lawrence-photo-hacking-privacy.

Chapter 5: Combating Cyber Attacks

23. "About The UnSlut Project," The UnSlut Project. www.unslutproject.com/about.html.

24. "Counter Speech," International Workshop on Misogyny and the Internet, Reagle, 2015. reagle.org/joseph/2015/07/counter-speech.html.

25. "Factsheet on the 'Right to Be Forgotten' Ruling," European Commission. ec.europa.eu/justice/data-protection/files/factsheets/factsheet_data_protection_en.pdf.

26. Lydia A. Jones, "Will California's Confusing New 'Online Eraser' Law for Minors Work?," *The Week*, January 2, 2015. theweek.com/articles/441431/californias-confusing-new-online-eraser-law-minors-work.

27. Quoted in Daniel F. Le Ray, "Advice from Revenge Porn Lawyer Carrie Goldberg," Whitman College, March 29, 2017. www.whitman.edu/newsroom/carrie-goldberg.

Chapter 6: The Future of Cyber Harassment

28. Andy Greenberg, "Inside Google's Internet Justice League and Its AI-Powered War on Trolls," *Wired*, September 19, 2016. www.wired.com/2016/09/inside-googles-internet-justice-league-ai-powered-war-trolls/.

29. Quoted in Kaitlyn Tiffany, "The Internet's Alt-Right Are Mistakenly Arguing with a Bot," *The Verge*, October 7, 2016. www.theverge.com/2016/10/7/13202794/arguetron-twitter-bot-alt-right-internet-bigots-4chan-sarah-nyberg.

30. Quoted in Tiffany, "The Internet's Alt-Right Are Mistakenly Arguing with a Bot."

31. Maeve Duggan, "5 Facts About Online Harassment," Pew Research Center, October 30, 2014. www.pewresearch.org/fact-tank/2014/10/30/5-facts-about-online-harassment/.

32. 18 U.S. Code § 2261A – Stalking. Legal Information Institute. www.law.cornell.edu/uscode/text/18/2261A.

33. Mary Traina, "Would the New Cyber-Harassment Bill Have Stopped My Stalker?," *The Cut*, March 24, 2016. www.thecut.com/2016/03/cybercrime-bill-wouldn-t-stop-my-stalker.html.

34. Traina, "Would the New Cyber-Harassment Bill Have Stopped My Stalker?"

DISCUSSION QUESTIONS

Chapter 1: The Rise of Cyber Mobs

1. What are some ways to stay safe while interacting with people on the Internet?

2. Why can anonymity be both a bad and good thing?

3. Why is it easy to get caught up in "mob mentality" or "groupthink"?

Chapter 2: Harassment Types

1. Why is cyberbullying harder to get away from than in-person bullying?

2. How are pictures used by cyber mobs to hurt a victim?

3. How does doxing someone make it easier for victims to be harassed in real life?

Chapter 3: Consequences of Cyber Attacks

1. Being the target of a cyber mob can make people lose what kind of opportunities?

2. In the case of the man who killed Cecil the lion, do you think the mob was doing a good thing or a bad thing?

3. Why do cyber mobs think it is ok to say hurtful things to others?

Chapter 4: Special Issues with Protected Groups

1. How can being a member of a protected group make someone a target of cyber mobs?

2. In the case of the reporter who was sent a video to give him a seizure, do you think the person who sent the video is guilty of trying to hurt the reporter?

3. Why do most people believe #Gamergate was about targeting women in the gaming industry?

Chapter 5: Combating Cyber Attacks

1. How can popups help the victims of cyberbullying?

2. After reading about the European Union (EU) and the "Right to Be Forgotten," what kinds of information should a person be able to erase from the Internet? What kinds of information, no matter how the individual feels about it, should remain available to other people through the Internet?

3. Do you think the Internet should censor hate speech?

Chapter 6: The Future of Cyber Harassment

1. What are some rules you think social networking websites could follow to stop cyber mobs from developing?

2. How could better training for law enforcement help defeat cyber mobs?

3. What should be the social norms for a good digital citizen?

Crash Override

help@crashoverridenetwork.com

www.crashoverridenetwork.com

Co-founded by Zoe Quinn, who was targeted during #Gamergate, Crash Override works with individuals affected by online harassment. The organization works with companies, governments, and other professionals to stop cyber mobs. Crash Override provides urgent help for individuals, as well as written guides and a network of outreach professionals. Victims can e-mail the organization to ask for help, and its website lists ways for individuals to get involved.

Cyber Civil Rights Initiative

(844) 878-CCRI

www.cybercivilrights.org

The Cyber Civil Rights Initiative was created by a former victim of online harassment. The website provides places for victims to share their stories, review resources, and connect with free legal assistance. The organization's toll-free helpline is open 24 hours a day, 7 days a week for victims of nonconsensual pornography to get advice and support.

The Megan Meier Foundation

515 Jefferson, Suite A

St. Charles, MO 63301

(636) 757-3501

www.meganmeierfoundation.org

The Megan Meier Foundation was started by Megan's mother after Megan committed suicide due to online harassment. It provides counseling services, workshops, and free presentations that are available on the website.

The National Center for Victims of Crime

2000 M Street NW, Suite 480
Washington, DC 20036
(202) 467-8700
victimsofcrime.org
The National Center for Victims of Crime is a nonprofit organization that advocates for victims' rights, trains professionals who work with victims, and serves as a trusted source of information on victims' issues. The mission of the National Center for Victims of Crime is to forge a national commitment to help victims of crime rebuild their lives.

The Tyler Clementi Institute for CyberSafety

104 West 29th Street, 4th Floor
New York, NY 10001
(646) 871-8095
tylerclementi.org/institute-for-cybersafety
The institute, part of New York Law School, works on cyber harassment cases pro-bono (without charge) for LGBT+ youth. It also trains lawyers to identify and fight against cyber mobs in the court system and provides legal resources for victims.

Books

Citron, Danielle Keats. *Hate Crimes in Cyberspace*. Cambridge, MA: Harvard University Press, 2014.
This book covers a wide range of topics, including how society and the Internet make harassment easier. Citron also covers civil rights, laws that can aid victims of cyber mobs, and free speech discussions.

Foxman, Abraham H., and Christopher Wolf. *Viral Hate: Containing Its Spread on the Internet*. New York, NY: Palgrave Macmillan. 2013.
Foxman and Wolf cover topics such as Internet hate, laws about hate speech, freedom of speech on the Internet, and working to reduce hate online. The book provides a number of appendices with good information on frequently asked questions, working to promote civil discussions, and advocacy.

Levmore, Saul, and Martha C. Nussbaum, eds. *The Offensive Internet*. Cambridge, MA: Harvard University Press, 2010.
This collection of essays about the Internet presents four distinct chapters: "The Internet and Its Problems," "Reputation," "Speech," and "Privacy." The essayists cover the range of abuses on the Internet, including problems of anonymity, false rumors, free speech, and privacy concerns.

Richards, Neil. *Intellectual Privacy: Rethinking Civil Liberties in the Digital Age*. New York, NY: Oxford University Press, 2015.
How does the Internet affect free speech and the exploration of ideas when it is monitored by both the government and media entities? Richards explains the debate on Internet privacy and the ways in which governments could react with new policy and legal precedents.

Ronson, Jon. *So You've Been Publicly Shamed*. New York, NY: Penguin, 2015.
Ronson spent three years meeting victims of high-profile public shamings. This book explores these victims' stories and the effects shaming had on them.

Waldron, Jeremy. *The Harm in Hate Speech*. Cambridge, MA: Harvard University Press, 2012.
Waldron discusses hate speech and its possible restrictions within the context of the First Amendment, as well as reasons why people think hate speech either should or should not be considered free speech.

Websites

Bystander Revolution
www.bystanderrevolution.org
This organization teaches people how to take action to stop cyberbullying. It includes actions people can take each week to fight bullying, tips from people who have been bullied about how to help a friend, and video interviews with celebrities about their experiences with bullying.

The Cyberbullying Research Center
cyberbullying.org
The Cyberbullying Research Center provides resources for teachers, law enforcement, parents, and students on Internet-based abuse. It provides original research and statistics, downloadable fact sheets on harassment and responses through the law, and firsthand accounts of victims of cyber bullying. There is a focus on prevention and the distribution of resources to aid those facing cyber mobs.

Digizen
www.digizen.org
Digizen is a website run by Childnet International, a nonprofit organization in the United Kingdom that works to protect children. The Digizen campaign focuses on teaching everyone how to be a better digital citizen.

Electronic Frontier Foundation (EFF)
www.eff.org
Founded in 1990, EFF defends civil liberties on the Internet. It focuses on freedom of expression, user privacy, policies, activism, and more. EFF especially concerns itself with ensuring that people's rights and freedoms are protected as society's use of the Internet increases.

NoBullying.com
www.nobullying.com
NoBullying.com has resources on cyberbullying, school bullying, and work bullying. The website is open to everyone as a free advice center. It was created as a social responsibility project for a company in Northern Ireland and now is one of the most consulted websites on bullying.

Working to Halt Online Abuse (WHOA)
www.haltabuse.org/about/about.shtml
WHOA, founded in 1997, provides education for the general public and law enforcement about online harassment. It also provides information about current laws that can be used to fight abuse.

INDEX

PICTURE CREDITS

ABOUT THE AUTHOR

Allison Krumsiek is an author and poet living in Washington, D.C. When she is not writing or editing, she can be found reading books or fearlessly defending her field hockey goal—but never at the same time. This is her second book for Lucent Press.